Drop-Out To Teacher

Overcoming Fear and Failure

WILLIAM J PALMER

E. Ce Miller

Editor

Jenna Privatsky

Graphic Designer

Thomas Balsamo Portrait Photographer

ISBN: 1500599948
ISBN 13: 9781500599942
Library of Congress Control Number: 2014913264
CreateSpace Independent Publishing Platform
North Charleston, South Carolina

$\mathcal{D}$EDICATED TO

my wife Jeanne,

my family,

and all those who inspired
the writing of this book

In Memory Of My Dear Friends

JOHN MARK TINETTI
(You were my memory and I miss you.)

And

DARLENE KAY RAYMOND

(Your legacy is that of courage and determination to everyone who knew and loved you. Your indomitable spirit will shine forever.)

SPECIAL THANKS TO

Emily Ce Miller

(Editor)

Jenna Privatsky

(Graphic Designer)

And

Jeanne Palmer

(Literary Consultant)

CONTENTS

The key to understanding what drives our emotions is to first accept that life's events are essentially neutral. Interpreting why we react to those events the way we do will lead to more effective emotional management.

There are times that present opportunities when we only have a moment to act.

Drop-Out To Teacher

Overcoming Fear and Failure

William J Palmer

WHY WRITE?

Over the course of my adult life students, colleagues and friends have encouraged me to write this book; encouraged me so enthusiastically that I too began to believe in the value of sharing my experiences. Once these expressions of encouragement reached a critical mass, I decided the time and effort involved in writing this book would be worth it, if it allowed me to offer insights that might help people strengthen their emotional management skills. But it really wasn't until I made a career change—the one I had pondered for so many years—that I began giving more consideration to the questions that begged answering: *what I would write* and *for what audience?*

I knew that someday I would leave the career I had chosen in order to become a teacher. My goal was not to teach the traditional subjects, but rather to instruct and counsel students with whom I shared formative coming-of-age experiences. I wanted to use my life experiences to generate meaningful instruction in a high school classroom. I wanted to teach students who had become chronic underachievers and who were at risk of not completing high school.

Therefore, in January of 1991, after meeting the business plan objectives for the client my two partners and I worked for, I decided it was the right time to make the career change I had pondered for a long time. I felt there was no time like the present to take the plunge—I left the world of commercial real estate development and brokerage to pursue my secondary education teaching credentials in both general and special education. I also began working as a substitute teacher at six different high schools.

As a teacher, I believe in positively impacting today's at-risk youth by creating an authentic, purposeful and meaningful learning environment. I believe that I can use my own life experiences as the building blocks for creating such an environment. I believe in my ability to affect positive change in the lives of some of the most disillusioned, disenfranchised and alienated high school students in my corner of the world. But little did I expect that when I finally decided to become a teacher I would end up teaching at the same high school I dropped out of twenty-four years before. After interviewing with my former high school—again, the one I had once dropped out of—I was offered a position to teach in both general and special education settings.

It didn't take me long to confirm what I had known about myself all along: that I had to teach students with whom I shared so many common experiences. I began my full-time teaching career in the department of Special Services in 1993. I have been an educator for over two decades and still have so much more to achieve.

Unsurprisingly, the questions of what I would write and for what audience were ultimately answered by some of the most important people in my life: my students. My students, more than anyone else, have supported my desire to write about the things we discuss in our classroom. Their insights and intuition continually amaze me. Their dignity in the face of tremendous adversity astounds me. Their understanding of the human condition is, at times, nothing less than profound.

These young people reward me with their honesty and they inspire me. Their unfettered enthusiasm in the face of insurmountable challenges reinforces my belief in both them and myself. They are an incredible group of young people who are trying to find purpose and meaning in their lives.

$\mathscr{E}$ARLY $\mathscr{A}$CTS OF $\mathscr{K}$INDNESS

$\mathscr{T}$his story begins back in the third grade, with a single act of kindness. My family had converted to Catholicism the summer before I began third grade. Then, my father moved us to New Jersey for a transfer assignment with his job. On my first day attending a Catholic school I remember the principal—a nun with the Sisters of Mercy—taking me by the hand and walking me to a classroom door at the end of a long, dark hallway. Class was in session so she knocked on the door and the instructor, Sister Mary Williams, walked out into the hall. The principal introduced me as a new student and asked Sister Mary if she would take me into her class. Sister Mary Williams took my hand and ushered me into the classroom. As I remember, I was the fifty-sixth third grader in her classroom that year. Imagine that today.

It is difficult to explain why this simple moment has had a lasting impact on me. I was a transfer student from a state a thousand miles away; a little boy who was a stranger to that school and that community and who had not made any friends yet. I think it was largely due to Sister Mary's unconditional acceptance of my young, third grade self. Her kindness that day is a memory and a lesson I bring with me into my classroom today—I refer to it as my "Sister Mary Williams' Syndrome"—calling on her compassion, understanding and insights into the emotional needs of her students when interacting with my own. Even today, when I am asked to accept another student into my charge or receive a request to add an additional student into one of my classes, I never turn that student away.

*A*nother early example of kindness in my academic life came from my high school speech teacher. Her name is Molly and she was a quintessential master teacher who understood that teaching goes beyond direct instruction. Molly understood that effective teaching involved identifying with and meeting the expectations of the students who were hers to educate. She was an educator who wasn't afraid to challenge the institution; both the academic institution in which she taught—an institution that she sensed was becoming increasingly irrelevant to the students she guided through high school during the Vietnam War—and the larger institution of a changing America given the unsettled times of the latter part of the 1960's.

The education I received from her taught me lessons that extended well beyond the skills I developed in how to effectively craft and deliver a speech. From the first day of class she inspired me with her passion for teaching and her understanding and compassion for the young people she taught. Molly is another teacher whose early lessons inform my own teaching methodology today—the relationships I form with my students as well as the lessons I strive to teach them; lessons that I hope extend to the challenges in their lives beyond the classroom.

A CHILDHOOD IN TURMOIL

With the exception of Sister Mary Williams, whose kindness became an inspiration for me, this was an ugly chapter in my life—filled with difficult emotions and frustrated curiosity; a time spent wondering about what life would be like if I'd been born into another family.

As difficult as it was I eventually accepted that thinking in those terms only advanced my belief that I was a victim, and that I had little-to-no power to change that. It is true that growing up I couldn't change the dysfunction within family—what I could control, however, was my ability to re-define my experiences as a source of wisdom and strength.

Redefining my life was a process fraught with challenges and facing them would not come until much later in life. At the time, all I could do was compare the lives my peers were living with my own, and imagine being part of another family.

Over the course of many years, I came to accept the challenges of changing my understanding of life's critical realities, determining that it was up to me to decide how I was going to frame and define my experiences, what value I was going to ascribe to them and how I was going to utilize them. I began to realize my potential by redeveloping a set of core beliefs about myself and the world around me. I determined that the only way I was ever going to get to where I wanted to be was by not allowing the adversity in my life to become a source of weakness. Instead of choosing to be a victim all my life, I found ways to use my adversity as a source of strength. I got to where I am today—a place of strength and self-fulfillment, in a career that I love—by utilizing the lessons to be found in all of my experiences, even the ugly ones. I made a series of life changing decisions that addressed one overreaching and fundamental of my formative years—that I could choose what my experiences of adversity were going to mean to me. I decided not to live my life as a victim.

This is the framework: about oneself, about lived experiences, and about the world, that I often focus on when working with my students. They also must define their experiences. They too must decide how to frame their experiences, and they too must decide where those experiences are going to take them. They too must decide whether or not to live the life of a victim.

My parents were not monsters. They were educated, caring and talented people, with intentions that were not rooted in evil. But their capacity to affect positive outcomes in their own lives and in the lives of their children was compromised by their lack of emotional management and effective problem solving skills.

Both of my parents grew up facing significant challenges; and I believe the challenges of their formative years influenced their adult lives. They were dealing with myriad unresolved issues, both intrapersonal and interpersonal conflicts that needed to be addressed, but never really were. Growing up, my parents struggled through the Great Depression. Their daily lives were challenged by both uncertainty and insecurity. Their families fought against the economic ruin of the 1930s—the scarcity of resources and general social uneasiness.

My father experienced the added challenge of being a first generation American—a child of Assyrian parents who had immigrated to the United States in 1913, from what was then Persia (modern day Iran). My father's family was very poor and uneducated; and American society and culture were completely foreign to them. Their only common thread to American society was their faith: they, as most of America, were Christians.

My grandfather worked hard, learned English and did his best to provide for his family. My grandmother never took to heart the benefit of learning English, so their Assyrian language was the language spoken in their home. My father learned the value of hard work and practiced this ethic by working his way through both college and law school. He often lamented that he did not own a dictionary until he was sixteen years old.

My mother's family came over on the "Mayflower", as the old expression goes. Family folklore says that my mother's maternal family was related to Nancy Hanks: Abraham Lincoln's mother. As of this writing I have only been able to trace my mother's ancestral roots back to her great, great grandmother: Effie Phoebe Hanks who was born circa 1857. So much more research needs to be done before family lore can be substantiated.

My mother was born in 1920 to an unwed teenager, making her birth socially and economically challenging for her mother, who lived in a very small community in central Illinois. In an era of Puritanically-informed family values there wasn't much compassion or empathy for my grandmother's predicament, which resulted in my mother growing-up without a stable family environment. She was taken in by her paternal grandmother until her single mother was able to accept the responsibility of raising her daughter.

The cost to each of my parents was that neither had consistent or relatable role models whose positive examples they could turn to when developing their own beliefs and behaviors. As a result, they grew into misguided and dysfunctional adults.

I remember, for example, when my father would agree to play catch with me—an experience that was a bit more complex and stress-filled than I imagine it was in other boyhood backyards. The first time I picked up a baseball my natural reaction was to pick it up with my left hand. From my father's perspective this was not a good idea—he was a man whose traditionally Assyrian beliefs taught him that being left handed was unacceptable. In Assyrian culture, the use of one's left hand was reserved for activities less sanitary than playing catch.

Ultimately, I was not left handed—only moderately ambidextrous—but the idea alone that I could be left handed was so abhorrent to my father that he refused to buy me a baseball glove designed for a left handed player. When we played catch I would try to play with the glove on my left hand, while throwing with my right, but it was completely unnatural for me. After switching the glove back and forth for a while I finally just started wearing it backwards on my right hand.

Although it took far longer than it should have, my father finally relented and purchased a left-handed glove for me—first a generic brand, but later the glove most young boys coveted: a Wilson A2000. It became a prized possession of mine.

A few years later my father constructed a basketball hoop and a homemade backstop in the alley behind our house. He had grown up playing pick-up games with his buddies at the schoolyard in his neighborhood and thought it would be nice if I could learn how to sink a basket. I did that left-handed too. With some humor I will just say… enough said.

My father tried—he really did; and I really wanted to have a good time tossing the ball back and forth with him. Oftentimes, in the end, it just wasn't worth seeing my father's frustration and disappointment. Out of these moments I try to construct a fond memory for myself, with the knowledge that at least my father tried to be there for me on those few afternoons when I could capture his attention, but his lack of understanding and the resulting intolerance over the years was just too much for me.

The cost was that in spite of our efforts, I was quickly being forced out of childhood. I was seeing a little too much of the world around me; certainly more than I was prepared to understand. I faced difficult choices in every area of my life, and those difficult choices were all I had from which to navigate my path.

There are formative moments in each of our lives and it is from these moments that we learn how to understand and manage our experiences. It seems to me that negative experiences are particularly challenging to manage. It is not necessarily the coping with the experience itself that is so difficult, but rather grappling with the beliefs that such events led us to develop about ourselves and the world around us. Witnessing an act of violence is certainly one such experience, and the processing of that violence, formative.

There were more afternoons—the kind when other children returned home from school to an attentive mother offering a snack, followed by homework or afternoon cartoons—when I would return home to a house of horrors; to a drunken, belligerent mother fighting with my father.

One afternoon I heard my parents fighting and ran upstairs to witness my father drag my mother into the shower, turn on the water and repeatedly bang her head against the shower wall. She was trying to fight him off as he was yelling obscenities. I tried to stop him, as I later would many more times, but I was a little boy and there wasn't much I could do except yell and cry and plead for him to stop. But he was not going to stop until he was done punishing her. There was screaming, swearing, blood streaming down the tile wall; both of my parents fully clothed and soaking wet.

Unfortunately, brutal as this scene was, it was only one of many incidents during what would become twenty-five years of terror: drinking and violence, police interventions, separations, divorce proceedings, orders of protection, ambulances in the driveway and so many futile efforts at sobriety and reconciliation that would, on so many levels, tear my family apart.

The feelings that build up in me from witnessing this violence at such a young age—feelings of loneliness, isolation, shame, embarrassment, confusion and anger—are the emotional memories that inform the work I do in my classroom, as I try to address my student's issues. Many of my students are experiencing the same emotional turmoil that I endured growing up, because their family structures are as fractured as mine was.

It was moments like these, and all those negative emotions that my family experienced, that prevented any of my six siblings—two older and two younger sisters and two younger brothers—and I from fully realizing our potential as students, as family members and as individuals. Outside of our tumultuous family life we were underachieving students and confused, angry young people.

Instead of having our natural abilities recognized and nurtured we were stripped of our youthful innocence; just one consequence of growing up in a home impacted by domestic violence. Instead of being guided into healthy and productive adulthoods, we grew up too fast and grappled with depression and insecurity. Our young lives, and the adulthoods that we grew into, were informed by the negative effects of guilt, shame and blame.

$\mathcal{L}$ESSON 1:
$\mathcal{U}$NDERSTANDING
$\mathcal{F}$ORMATIVE $\mathcal{M}$OMENTS

*I*t is clear that each of us will experience formative events throughout our lives—but what is more crucial than the event itself, is the opportunity it affords us to personally reflect upon that event, and decide how it will form us, moving forward. Such opportunities strengthen our emotional resiliency, offering us a moment of pause in which to examine our beliefs about an event, and how it has affected us. While negative experiences are challenging to manage, the potential for these experiences to negate our potential can be devastating.

It is not necessarily the process of coping with an experience itself that is so difficult, but rather understanding the beliefs we develop about ourselves and the world around us, in the wake of a formative, often traumatic, event. Witnessing an act of violence is certainly one such event, and the processing of that violence, formative. But understanding how we process the experiences in our lives is the key to then understanding, and better managing, our reactions to those experiences.

The problem is that most of us don't think about our thinking—we end up blaming events, other people and/or world conditions for any challenges we may face in our lives. What is crucial to developing a more rational way of responding to our experiences is recognizing that how we process and then give meaning to our experiences is what causes our emotional reactions, not the experience itself.

Each of us has the ability to control our reactions to the experiences in our lives. We have control over our quality of life and we have the ability to effectively manage our own thoughts and behaviors when processing our life experiences. The experiences themselves are neutral. We give them meaning by assigning them value.

So the question is: *how do you want to live your life?* Do you want to live by blaming your life experiences for your behaviors, or do you want to take control of your life by effectively managing your emotional responses to the things that happen to you?

When working with my high school students, this is where I often get the most resistance. We have been socialized to believe that our reactions to experiences are because of the experience itself. This belief is distorted and self-serving. I have found that most irrational thinkers do have an underlying rationality that allows them to recognize the ineffectiveness of their own thinking; and that those who resist responding to their life experiences with rational thought do so because intuitively they know that doing so means they will have to change their behaviors. Many students are too insecure to commit to changing their thinking, as the prospect of having to subsequently change their behavior is daunting.

ℰARLY ℭONSEQUENCES

*A*s shocking as the shower scene was to my young life, it was just one of many unforgettable scenes of domestic violence that my siblings and I witnessed as we grew up. My mother would get drunk while my siblings and I were in school and my father was at work. At some point during his work day my father would talk to my mother on the phone and realize she had been drinking. Often, he would come home early to mete out her punishment while we were still in school.

Unfortunately, I would sometimes return home from school early. One afternoon I found my father pinning my mother to the floor in the foyer of our home, beating her with closed fists. He was on top of her, punching her breasts and yelling profanities as she was trying to fight him off. She was screaming and crying but powerless to fend off his attack—helpless because of her size and because she was intoxicated.

After realizing I was home, standing right behind him screaming in horror, my father pushed me out of the way and continued beating my mother. I regained my footing and stood beside them, trying to stop my father's fists from landing blows. He finally regained control of his rage and stopped. At that point I only remember running. Out to the back yard, maybe. I was so traumatized by what I had witnessed, so hysterical; that what immediately followed is really just a blur.

Witnessing domestic violence at such a young age had a profoundly negative impact on my intrapersonal self and on my relationship with my parents. I despised my father for his brutality and I wanted to protect my mother, but there wasn't anything I could do about either. The alcohol abuse and violence were escalating in their intensity.

My negative feelings about myself and the people around me, as well as my sense of security, were tenuous. I had already witnessed too much violence—and not the stuff you see on TV. Mine occurred without any stunt people. It was the real thing and it was going on live, unrehearsed and unedited in any given room of my family's home.

Reflecting on the conditions I grew up under, I see that I had been backed into a defensive position and my chosen defense was anger. I became an angry, tough kid—or at least emulated the persona of a tough kid. My anger was clearly a defense mechanism, but it was also a statement of rebellion.

Any youthful innocence I might have had was replaced with helplessness and hopelessness—feelings that were grounded in fear and a sense of failure that stemmed from my inability to alter the dynamics of my family. I was forced out of childhood too quickly, and saw a little too much of the world around me; certainly more than I was prepared to understand.

Compounding my destructive familial experiences were the negative dynamics of my social environment—an environment directly impacted by the struggles going on at home. I faced difficult choices in every area of my life, and those difficult choices were all I had from which to navigate my path.

I was angry and confused and felt drained of both energy and potential—a complex mixture of emotions that only served to foster my growing rebellion. I became a "greaser". You know the type: James Dean in *Rebel without a Cause* or John Travolta in *Grease* or Judd Nelson in *The Breakfast Club*—except I was a lot younger than the characters portrayed in those movies.

I smoked my first cigarette in the third grade, from a pack I had stolen from a corner store in Sea Bright, New Jersey. We had recently moved to Rumson, New Jersey from a Chicago suburb, I was 9 years old, and I'd set out that Saturday morning, along with a group of neighborhood boys with whom I had become friends, intent on stealing a pack of cigarettes (and buying ice cream and candy).

As I reflect back on the decisions I made—the style I embraced and the lifestyle I pursued, it is apparent that my choices were rooted in my own hopelessness, helplessness and powerlessness. I was trying to compensate for living in an insane situation, with little to no control over the events that occurred within my family. I couldn't become a respectful and dutiful son within my dysfunctional family structure. I was way too confused and way too angry. Just like many of my students today, I felt justified in my anger and growing discontent.

CHANGED BOY

*I*t was during my Mother's post-partum depression, after the birth of her fourth child, that she began her long struggle with alcohol abuse. Her depression brought to the surface many years of anger and frustration, and the sense of helplessness that stemmed from growing up as the only child of an unwed, teenage mother.

As I noted earlier, my grandmother was seventeen when she gave birth to my mother. She had no means of supporting herself, while my biological grandfather's own emotional issues eventually led to his institutionalization in an Illinois state run hospital. It wasn't until early adolescence, that my grandmother was finally capable of accepting more parental responsibility for my mother.

It was those early years of uncertainty, insecurity and loss that interfered with my mother's ability to develop a strong sense of self-worth and the skills necessary for personal independence. If she had grown up in a nurturing environment that fostered her potential, perhaps she might have developed the inner strength that comes from a positive sense of self-worth—qualities that would have served her well in her adult life, and especially in her marriage.

Despite these challenges, my mother was an extraordinary woman. She was a beautiful woman and she learned to hide her insecurities behind her beauty. She was also a very talented singer and she loved opera in particular. I mean, she had *a voice*—a raw talent that was recognized when she was a teenager and cultivated by her classical music voice and singing instructors. She devoted every waking breath to her musical practice, until she was on the verge of performing with what would later become the Lyric Opera in Chicago.

Through her music, my mother finally began to develop a sense of purpose. Then she met my father. She wasn't ready for the courtship that ensued, but my father was a determined man who knew what he wanted; and he wanted my mother on his arm. He pursued her until she fell for him. Instead of pursuing her dream, she married and began contributing to the Baby Boom. She became confined to suburban lifestyle—a whole new way of life in the years following World War II, especially for a city girl.

She began living an antiseptic life in an all-white, middle class community where being an at-home mom was the expectation of the times; and where she was suffocated by a controlling husband with traditional Middle Eastern Assyrian values.

This new, unfamiliar reality compounded her sense of isolation. Her dreams of singing professionally were extinguished and her life started to spin out of control. As the years passed her emotional needs continued to be set aside by a husband who was insensitive to her desires; she continued drinking, and that drinking intensified.

*I*t is due to my experience of witnessing my mother's alcohol abuse that I struggle with the idea that alcoholism is a disease—I don't, in fact, believe that alcoholism is a disease at all. I don't subscribe to the suggestion that there are biological factors that predispose certain people to alcohol addiction—I don't believe, for instance, that my mother couldn't help her drinking and was not in control of her own decisions to drink, because she had a disease.

Instead, I think this kind of belief only enables the alcohol abuser to descend further and further into their own victimhood. Dismissing alcoholism as nothing more than an uncontrollable disease, I think, diminishes our own individual autonomy over our lives and our life choices. It suggests that we are victims of random circumstance, rather than encouraging strong, assertive, positive and productive decision-making.

I don't believe my mother was a victim of her biology—rather, she was a desperately frustrated woman who, in order to grapple with the misery she experienced in her marriage, decided to medicate that misery with alcohol and used that alcohol as a way to repudiate my father's need for control.

I don't share this belief with the intent of alienating or offending anyone dealing with their own experiences of alcohol abuse—either their personal substance abuse or the substance abuse of someone close to them. Rather, I hope to emphasize the belief that we all have the power to control our actions in positive, healthy and productive ways.

We are not victims of predetermined circumstance. We are empowered individuals in control of whether or not the choices we make are hurtful or harmful, are going to lead us towards realizing our full potential, or are only going to drive us further away from growing into our best selves.

⌣⌐

My mother was, at the very least, lonely in her marriage, and her deep-seated resentment and anger continued to intensify. Her relationship with my father was not a balanced one—especially compared to today's expectations of equal partnerships. Autocratic would be a more accurate description of their marriage, and my father was the autocrat. Ultimately my mother would have an affair and I strongly suspect that my father had one too.

My parent's issues with infidelity came to a head one Sunday morning when my father and I were driving in the car alone. He wanted to glean some information from me about my mother, and ultimately he manipulated me into exposing a short affair my mother had with a house painter my father had hired.

I was the first of my siblings to wake one morning, and in the kitchen I found my mother in a full-body embrace with the house painter— a passionate, open mouthed kiss that seemed to me to last an eternity. I stopped in my tracks, stunned for a long moment before I realized it was my mother and the painter—she was having an affair with the house painter!

Within a few days my mother left with the painter while my father was away on business, and my seventeen-year-old sister took over while my mother was gone. Though my mother was seeking greater meaning in her life by engaging in an extra-marital affair, she quickly realized that it was not leading her where she wanted to go. She returned before my father did, having reconsidered the affair. She came into my bedroom, late that night and gave me a kiss. We never talked about her leaving and she never knew what I had witnessed. My siblings and I made an unspoken promise to never divulge the affair to our father.

But that morning in the car, my father asked me some leading questions that ended with him saying "So things have been a lot better around the house lately, now that your mother hasn't been drinking." I innocently, but stupidly, said: "Yeah things have been a lot better since she came back". That was it. He raced home, stormed into the house and locked himself and my mother in the kitchen. After a brutal day-long battle of recriminations and admonitions, I was ultimately found responsible for exposing her secret. It was a startling moment; I was blamed for being outsmarted by my father, who, suspecting something had changed but unable to put his finger on what, figured his nine-year-old son could be tricked into telling him.

That evening my mother confronted me. She knelt down until she was eye-level with me, shaking my shoulders and crying and screaming: "How could you tell?" and "What were you thinking? Do you know what you've done?"

I left the house in hysterics, got on my bike and rode the neighborhood streets looking for a friend, but there was none to be found. By then it was dinner time and my friends were probably sitting down at the dinner table with their families, while I was riding the lonely streets of the neighborhood, trying to get a grip on myself and on what was happening to me.

But then it hit me—a moment of depressing clarity. I was stuck in an insane situation—and *I was the kid*! My parents' relationship was *not my fault* and *it was wrong of them to blame me*. I was hurt, confused and angry. The last thing I wanted to do was to go home again, but I was nine; it's not like I had much of a choice. I went home a changed boy that night.

Although my parents reconciled again, this was a turning point for me. I had lost even more respect for my parents, and I had lost my sense of belonging. I had lost what little sense of security I had left, and my sense of self-worth had been stripped away. My resiliency was tested again.

Resiliency is remarkable—it is a powerful defense but it can also be a powerful offense. In my case, I went on the offensive for the rest of what remained of my childhood.

⌣⟶

*D*espite all the turmoil, my father took it upon himself to try to teach me the multiplication tables—an idea that didn't work out very well. My father had his own method of teaching, and in this case it was that I *should* be able to learn the multiplication tables at *his* pace—over the course of a single weekend. He spent the next two days frustrated and angry that I was not meeting his expectation of my learning at the pace he demanded.

He made negative comments and asked questions like: "How can you be my son and not be able to learn this?" At one point he called my mother into the room to ask her if she knew why I was unable to learn what he was trying to teach me. I don't remember her exact response, but I do believe she was supportive of me.

When I went to school on Monday I was not the same boy who had been introduced to Sister Mary Williams on the first day of third grade. I was never going to be that boy again. My sense of self had been shaken. I became a chronic underachiever; part of the permanent lower tier of academic underachievers, and my peer relationships were an extension of my academic failures.

I gravitated toward social situations that were reflective of my academic standing and affiliated with students to whom I could most relate—the discouraged, disenfranchised and alienated. They were the same students who I would eventually stand before as a teacher—students just like me who hated school, hated their family and hated themselves; and who let the world around them know it.

$\mathcal{L}$ESSON 2:
$\mathcal{A}$DDRESSING
$\mathcal{R}$EBELLION AND
$\mathcal{U}$NDERACHIEVEMENT

When I relate the story of my father and the multiplication tables to my students they often groan or offer an awkward laugh—because they get it. They understand that those moments with my father had a profound impact on the way I perceived myself as a person, family member and student.

I tell this story to my students because we often explore the moment that school started turning south for them. When did they start losing interest in the educational experience? I tell them that for me it was sometime between the first and third grade, when it became clear that I was definitely reading below grade level and had no support at home. My potential was being thwarted and there was a growing disparity between my abilities and my academic achievement.

For students, resisting achievement is often rooted in a fear of expectations. The fear that as one gets a better handle on things, peoples' expectations for them will heighten, evolving into greater demands for higher levels of achievement. There can be a tendency to ratchet-up the pressure on students. Expressions like: "You got a B on that test, that's great!" followed by: "Just think, by working only a little harder you could have gotten an A". A celebration of achievement suddenly becomes an expression of heightened expectations. Emotionally this student feels knocked down.

I use this as an example for why so many students are okay with underachievement, and my students know exactly what I am talking about. They will do anything to avoid that kind of pressure, including just (barely) passing their classes. For many, underachieving is preferable to the pressure of being compared to others or being pressured for not maintaining higher achievement levels.

Why do so many young people facing adversity often react in self-defeating ways? Their reasoning has to do with a sense of powerlessness—one of the primary causes of anger. Reacting angrily is a way for such students to feel a sense of power. I have a theory about students who become rebellious and who choose lifestyles that are threatening to peers and adults alike. I believe that they are no longer searching for meaning and purpose in their lives because they have already rejected everything—a lifestyle choice rooted in anger and powerlessness.

Some students who turn to dark and angry modes of self-identification and behavior have, based on their outward appearance, decided to detach from the mainstream. While I was growing up the identity of rebellion was that of the "greaser"—in the same way students today might identify as "emo" or "gothic".

A well-known example of this is Judd Nelson's character in the movie *The Breakfast Club*—the Criminal. When I show this movie in the anger management class I teach, students are always able to identify the character I relate to most—of course, the Criminal.

Why had such an intelligent young man become such a behavior problem? Why did he have so much anger? What were the influences that led him to shutting down? Clearly, he was very capable. So why didn't he, in the face of adversity, choose to become the star of the diving team, or the editor of the school newspaper, or captain of the football team, or class president? Why didn't he simply choose to become the student he was intellectually capable of becoming? Why did his young life become a race to the bottom?

The "Criminal" knew how to exhibit a persona of power through intimidation. He was skilled at being a menace and was able to emotionally distance himself from the social structures that, while rejecting, he still had to live within. His defense was to play offense. He masked the pain of unresolved issues and internal conflicts by becoming an aggressive, unforgiving and defiant juvenile delinquent. He used his created persona to compensate for feelings of inadequacy, insecurity, loneliness and powerlessness. He could have been a student in my classroom. The challenge is to seek a greater understanding for why a student has disengaged as a learner. Why they have rendered themselves unavailable? Examine the word *available*. It is actually two words right? A student is not *able* if he or she will not *avail* themselves. Similarly, *availability* is also two words: we don't have the *ability* if we will not *avail* ourselves. So the key is to identify the irrational thoughts that are causing a student's behavior and then replace those thoughts with more rational ways of thinking, so as to have the best chance at cognitive ability level achievement.

When I'm working with my students and we're sharing thoughts on some of the underlying reasons for their rebellion and underachievement, there is often a common, emotion-based thread that runs through their decision-making. Many students struggle with a fear of failure, but just as many—if not more—fear success (or both) as well. If they're being honest with themselves, students will acknowledge that they'd do just about anything else rather than give their parents, teachers or anyone in a position of authority reason to feel satisfied over their behavior. Many of the negative behaviors at-risk youth develop have to do with validation—the last thing a child is going to do is validate their parent's dysfunctional behavior by meeting their expectations. I know this because I felt the same way.

We all have defense mechanisms, but the students I teach have worked to develop theirs more than most. They have become well-guarded and built emotional fortresses around themselves designed to keep others at bay. Often, in addition to those emotional obstacles is their belief—as I experienced—that any success they have, or that you have helped them gain, is a victory for you and a loss for them.

Growing up I certainly wasn't going to validate the adults in my life by behaving in ways they would have found satisfactory. In the case of my parents, doing so would have felt like I was sanctioning their destructive behavior. At the time, choosing to rise above my parent's reckless behavior would have felt as though I were saying their behavior was not negatively impacting me, when it clearly was. It would have felt as though I were saying: *don't worry about me, I'm going to be okay*—but that wasn't the reality of the situation.

For most struggling youth, anger and rebellion are power. Young people use this anger and rebellion as ways of defending themselves against people who they believe don't understand their experiences. I am living testimony of how misdirected and self-defeating this coping skill can be. I suffered the negative consequences of my own actions; and this pattern is one I see in the lives of my students. There is no denying the correlation between a dysfunctional family structure, rebellion and low academic achievement.

One essential element for student and teen success is healthy student-teacher (or student-parent) relationship, built on a foundation of respect. When a teenager realizes his or her relationship with their teacher or parent is based on respect for who they are as an individual, they are better able to strengthen their sense of respect for themselves.

Self-respect is a cornerstone of effective decision making and productive living. As a teenager begins to develop their own understanding of self-respect, it's important to respond to their processes with patience, attentiveness and sympathy. It's critical to avoid being dismissive of a teen because their current growth experience doesn't fit in with your own agenda for the moment. Body language is critical at these times too—we can't be looking at the clock, or down at our desk, or shuffling papers. When a teenager begins to grow into their own sense of self-respect it is a very empowering experience—both for the teen themselves and for their teacher or parent.

I shared one such experience with a young man enrolled in one of the classes I was teaching towards the end of my eleventh year as an educator. This student had been an underachiever his entire academic life, even though he had an above-average IQ. In fact his IQ score landed in the low-superior range (as did those of his two older brothers) yet he was a D-average student.

The origins of this student's dysfunction lay in the fact that he had such talented older brothers; his thoughts were rooted in a fear of failure and a fear of success. He couldn't bear the idea of being compared to his brothers, and failing to measure up to their success, so he simply didn't apply himself to begin with. He had convinced himself that if he didn't try then he couldn't be compared to his two older brothers; the way he saw it, not trying meant not risking failure. Trying and not doing as well as his brothers, however, would be a failure.

He also believed that even when working at his ability level his achievements wouldn't compare to those of his brothers. He was convinced that he wouldn't be able to sustain the effort necessary for high-achievement, as his brothers had. While he may never be as successful as his brothers, neither would he be a failure since he had never tried to succeed to begin with. This student had spun himself quite a web.

Once I believed he was open and ready to hear my input, I spoke to him about this. Apparently, no one had ever been as blunt as I was in identifying the issues he was facing. I'll never forget the look on his face, when I put words to his internal experience, and expressed that I understood all he was feeling—he was shocked.

This was a powerful moment for both of us—for him as a student and a young man, and for myself as an educator. I had struck a chord in his consciousness—validating him by shedding light on his set of core beliefs and discussing them with him without judgement. He honored my patience and dedication by suggesting I share my hard-earned wisdom with others—and this moment was one of my inspirations for ultimately writing a book. Unfortunately, while this particular young man did take steps towards improving his academic achievement, he never came close to realizing his full potential.

In the last scene of *The Breakfast Club*—my favorite—no words are spoken. In this scene the Criminal shares a moment of compassion and understanding with the girl he secretly admired, and as the film ends viewers are left with the image of him walking across the football field, raising his fist into the air.

I think everyone can understand what he was feeling: a tremendous sense of personal satisfaction; an acceptance that he had not felt for a long time, if ever. He was experiencing a sense of personal fulfillment because he had been accepted for who he was and not for how he behaved, by someone who he valued. He was beginning to realize his own self-worth. That is what makes that last scene so powerful: we all want to realize our own value and we celebrate it when we do.

$\mathcal{A}$ $\mathcal{F}$AMILY IN $\mathcal{D}$ENIAL

$\mathcal{M}$y father used to tell me not to let what was happening in the family ruin my life. He knew the negative impact it was having on his children, especially on me, and yet he only said that I shouldn't let it "ruin me".

Let it *ruin me*? I remember thinking: *are you kidding me?* I wish I could have shaken some sense into him. I wish I had said: *look around Dad; at me and your other children. We are a train wreck.* I wish I could have confronted him, challenged him to recognize that none of his children were realizing their potential or tapping into their talents. None of us ever did while we were growing up. Instead, we were dirty, insecure, confused, angry, underachieving children being robbed of our innocence and stripped of our potential by having our abilities ignored. We were imprisoned in an insane situation that perpetuated our confusion, anger, depression and underachievement.

My siblings and I only had each other as we would huddle and cower together under the force of a frequently brutal father and an alcohol-abusing mother. We were incapable of overcoming the adversity that surrounded us. I wasn't capable of compliance or ability level achievement, even if I had wanted that. I hadn't developed the resources that would have given me the "bootstraps" to do so.

Even if I had miraculously been born with extraordinary talents and innate abilities that gave me the wherewithal to withstand the frequent emotional assaults and succeed in the face of so much adversity, I was still incapable of giving my parents the satisfaction and sense of public pride of having a compliant and achieving first born son. I was way too angry to succeed or—as it seemed to me then—to give them any victories. Instead, I raced to the bottom, and became successful at failing.

In my adult life, personal reflection has become a powerful tool I use to better understand human dynamics and social interactions. When I compare the decisions I made growing up to those my students make today, it reinforces my belief that familial environments have a profound impact on the choices young people make, and the lifestyles they choose. When those familial environments are filled with conflict and adversity, young people are driven towards making almost always negative and self-defeating choices.

Humans require nurturance and consistent guidance. We cannot be neglected or abused or abandoned without it having a deleterious impact on one's sense of self.

My father's expectations were consistent with his beliefs about compliance, achievement and the role of family, but these beliefs were inconsistent with the principles of sound child rearing and demonstrated his fundamental misunderstanding of the stages of child development.

He often looked to his friends and saw the progress their children were making and he didn't like what he saw when he compared them to the progress that his children were making. What my father didn't recognize was that his friends were raising their children through consistent parental guidance and nurturance.

My father's approach to child rearing and marital partnership was a reaction to many of his own unrecognized shortcomings: his fear of being judged and his sense of inferiority as the child of immigrant parents who had little, if any, formal education. The fear that these feelings created was deep-seated and grew from his own insecurities over his perceived judgements from others.

My father had a paranoid view of his own personal value and self-worth; and about how he fit into his perceived roles within the family and society. This caused him a tremendous amount of frustration and inner turmoil. The more situations, events and life conditions grew out of his control, the more he felt the need to assert control. His perceived need to assert control, amplified by his personal frustration, confusion and anger only allowed the events of his life to spiral out of control even more.

That kind of distorted thinking had a devastating effect on our family dynamics, and was a fundamental character flaw that led to many of my father's failures as the patriarch of the family. After examining my father's life from the perspective of my own adult life, I have come to believe that his most fundamental emotional need was his desire for absolute control.

My father's absolute need to control the beliefs and behaviors of others, his mistaken and misguided notion that power would deliver his desired outcome, his self-defeating and terribly distorted thought processes and his behaviors were largely what sent our family into a free fall. As children, we saw our parental role models engaged in a never-ending power struggle; and were unable to control anything ourselves.

The more one tries to control events, environments, or behaviors, the less control one often actually has. As a teacher this was a painful, but critical lesson for me to learn. I had to learn that control is not mine for the taking just because as a teacher I hold a position of authority. I learned how to tell the difference between knowing when to influence a given situation or behavior of my students and when to let them sort out a situation on their own.

My father would have benefitted from understanding this concept; allowing himself to let go of his control issues as he grew through his adult life. Instead, he fostered resentment and animosity in his household. Today my surviving siblings are still struggling with the negative effects of guilt, shame and blame.

When facing her struggling and isolated children my mother would rationalize and justify her decisions and behaviors by proclaiming that her children would be okay. Both my parents were living in denial. But that is the insidious power of denial: we convince ourselves that despite our dysfunctional behaviors everything will be okay.

⌒

Later, my father moved us back to the same house we lived in before moving to New Jersey. At first this seemed like an opportunity for a positive turning point—picking up where I had left off with my early childhood friends. After returning to my old neighborhood, my friends encouraged me to join them in playing little league baseball and at their Saturday morning bowling league; all the standard rites of passage for a middle-class, suburban boy.

But I moved through the process of growing up with a heavy heart, because of the madness of my home life; and it was becoming more complicated. I didn't have much support beyond my neighborhood friends. I think my father came to three of my baseball games over the three years that I played, and he didn't approve of my joining the bowling team, citing that it was a "blue collar" sport and therefore beneath our social class.

To be fair, perhaps my father didn't really know how to be more involved. As the son of immigrant parents, there were few opportunities for children to participate in organized activities when he was a boy. He didn't have a role model from whom to learn how to be a role model beyond the value of hard work, which he learned from his father. But his lack of involvement was yet another wedge driven between our rapidly deteriorating relationship.

Those years took me from fifth to seventh grade. During this time I also worked mowing a neighbor's lawn for three dollars a week and delivering newspapers for the local news agency. I really had to push my father to let me have those jobs, since he took it as an affront to his ability to provide for his family—the furthest thing from my mind. I was just trying to do what other boys were doing. It also got me out of the house and gave me the opportunity to build self-reliance skills.

Unfortunately, I was also stealing from my parents, the neighborhood stores and once a friend and I even broke into a neighbor's house to steal from their child's savings jar. We got caught for that burglary and were charged with breaking and entering. I was placed on probation, and my mother was able to hide it from my father as I paid full restitution to the victim with my lawn mowing and newspaper money. It was not a very proud moment for me, but rather a warning sign of where I was headed.

I was living a dual life—trying to remain friends with the kids I had been friends with before moving to New Jersey, while still seeking out new kids that shared my feelings of confusion and anger. The forces of the latter group won out and I slowly moved away from my early childhood friends.

My parents continued the drinking and violence, and I gravitated toward the tougher students attending my Catholic school. That school was another compounding factor in my drifting away from those early childhood friends. Those guys attended the local public school, so they were also no longer my classmates as they had been when I attended the same school. That separation was more than I could handle socially. As I moved beyond grade school, I had no choice but to cultivate new friendships from my new group of classmates. I began building a new foundation and social group.

I went on to meet new students, which wasn't all bad because some of them became very close friends—including two who stood up at my wedding. As a testament to how powerful those first childhood friends were to me as well, two of them also attended my wedding and I attended theirs. Even after nearly twenty years we knew the importance of sharing those special days, and included each other in those celebrations.

*I*t wasn't always easy though. I'll never forget the regret I felt at the wedding of one of those early childhood friends, when the mother of the groom asked me what had happened to me all those years before, when I began to grow more distant from that first group of boyhood friends. I wasn't able to give her a clear answer. She never really knew why I grew further and further away from those friends, and at that moment I chose not to try to explain it to her. It was a sad moment for me. There were just too many differences between us—too much shame about my young past and the dynamics within my family, and too many secrets I believed I had to keep.

Coincidentally, many years later, when I was completing my student teaching, the daughter of one of these childhood friends was a student in the class I was teaching. My friend had a very unusual last name, and when I discovered this same name on my class roster I asked the student what her father's first name was. Sure enough, it was my old friend.

We got together once after that to share memories and stories; to try and catch up, but even then as two adults we could not bridge the gap between his life experiences and mine. It was the last time I saw him. Today I would still love to be able to explain what had happened to me all those years ago, and consequently, to our friendship.

$\mathcal{D}$ ROPPING $\mathcal{O}$ UT

$\mathcal{A}$lthough the experience of changing schools and being forced to make new friends wasn't all bad, that transition still led me to cementing my identity as a tough guy—at least in my own mind. I really wasn't that tough. I continued to hang out at the bowling alley, but instead of bowling I went into the adjacent pool hall, to play dollar call ball. I won some and lost some.

The point here is that I began to build new relationships with a tougher group of young men and women who were considerably older than I was. But I was able to pull it off because I was mature for my age and looked older. I was pretty good at projecting a tough, older image—I was even getting served at a local liquor store at sixteen. Unfortunately, that tougher edge wasn't hard to achieve, because it was rooted in my growing inner rage.

During this time I was able to land another job for the news agency. I was still in the newspaper business, but this one was hawking newspapers at the intersection outside the bowling alley, between lanes of stopped traffic. I sold the *Chicago American* and the *Chicago Daily News*—both long since out of business.

Back then newspapers were published twice a day, giving me an early morning and early evening job. I would walk down the street between stopped cars, yelling: "get your *Chicago American*, get your *Daily News*" with a canvas change pouch tied around my waist. It was a great gig that taught me about getting to work on time and working hard. It was another lesson in self-reliance.

That job was also an important stepping-stone in my social life. When the boy I sold papers with offered me a hand-me-down set of wooden-wheeled roller skates, I was introduced to the sport of indoor roller-skating and a new social horizon opened up for me. I remember seeking out girls to skate with, sometimes holding hands while skating: fond memories indeed.

Within a year there were two new pool halls in town: The Royal Cue and The Eight Ball. I spent all of my free time at those pool halls, at the expense of the roller rink. The attraction had faded, since the lure of the pool hall spoke to my attitude about myself. I was at a juncture where I had to make a decision, and I chose the pool hall.

By hanging out with a group of kids two, three, and four years older than I was, I learned social skills beyond my years; skills that aided my pursuit to grow up as fast as I possibly could. They were angry, tough guys—and they had accepted me.

The lure of the bad guy image was too great and my need to be seen as a bad guy was too strong. My rebellion was a compensatory behavior for the insecurities that stemmed from my confusion and anger. I knew that the people I was hanging around with were not going to be accepted by my parents and that was also part of their appeal.

I continued my race to the bottom while using my dysfunctional family as an excuse. I had settled on the idea that I was failing because of my parents, and there was no one to guide me in any other direction—not that I would have listened if there had been. It was too late. I had made my choices and I wasn't going to listen to anyone who may have tried to guide me otherwise.

One of the more significant shifts I made during that critical time was to become friends with one of the toughest families in town—a family of three brothers who were feared by almost everyone. The youngest brother was my age; the other two were several years older. They hung out in a couple of rooms carved out of the basement of their mother's home, and once I was accepted into their little clan I spent a lot of time hanging out with them.

The first time I got drunk was at their place, drinking Pinch scotch whiskey. I got wasted that night and figured I was pretty much screwed when I got home. Instead, when I walked into the house, through the back door and into the kitchen, both of my parents were there and didn't have a clue that their fourteen year old son was drunk. They were also under the influence. That night was the beginning of a new chapter. I began drinking on a fairly regular basis throughout high school.

These were the guys with whom I so desperately wanted to be identified. These were the guys I wanted to emulate and hang out with. I had come to a fork in the road, and decided how I really wanted to live my life. Then I experienced another life changing event that shook me to my very core.

While my mother had a lot of unresolved issues that caused turmoil in her life and in the lives of her children, she was also a sensitive, thoughtful and reflective soul who instilled in me some basic beliefs about the value of all life; and taught me to treasure the beauty of nature.

Through the pressures of peer influences, I violated that belief structure one day by taking part in the senseless destruction of several song birds similar to the ones my mother and I would marvel at upon their return each spring. I'd felt pressured to do so, and was disgusted with myself for acting in direct opposition to what I had been taught to believe by killing these beautiful songbirds. I had sunk to the bottom of my life experiences. But this also served as a huge lesson: never again would I compromise my values in such a destructive way in an effort to impress someone else. Never again would I compromise my values in order to be accepted.

I betrayed myself that afternoon because of a distorted belief that I had to impress others. I knew I had a long way to go to heal from that afternoon's events. But one thing I also realized on the long walk home that afternoon was that I couldn't hang out with those guys again. When I walked off their property that day it was for the last time.

I relate this story to the students in my Social Interactions course because it is a powerful lesson that I had to learn about the toll ethical and moral betrayals take on the spirit. I still cringe over the idea that I admired these guys. Underneath it all I knew that I wasn't being true to myself. But I was willing to deny what I knew because the image I had created for myself was more important to me.

The day when I knew I had completely violated my own values in order to maintain that image was a profound day of reckoning. I couldn't live with myself for a long time after that. I share this story with my students because I want them to avoid the kinds of negative experiences that come from collapsing under the pressure of peer influences.

At that point I was no longer trying to be a decent student. Instead, I was just going through the motions. My freshman year turned out to be my last year in Catholic schools. My parents enrolled me in a Catholic high school for boys, which was outside our immediate area, and I didn't have a single friend joining me for the ninth grade.

At the end of the school year I informed my parents that I would not be returning to that school. The school apparently did not want me back either. I ended up at my district public high school for tenth grade, along with my two closest friends who had also been removed from the Catholic school they attended that year. For the next two years the three of us built quite a reputation for ourselves—pursuing as much hedonism as possible. We developed a wider circle of friends over time, and together we partied our way into our early adult lives. Sadly, those two guys with whom I shared so many life experiences and who were two of the young men who stood up at my wedding are now deceased; both tragedies from life's choices.

By that time I pretty much ignored everything my father had to say, and when he chose to speak to me it was mostly in criticisms. My parents' drinking and the violence never let up, and I tried to distance myself from a lot of it, except as it impacted my younger siblings, or if I had to separate my parents during a fight. I still had a sense of responsibility to protect my mother and siblings, but I wish I had done more.

The dysfunction in my home had become so great that there was little meaningful communication between my parents and me. I was burned out and wanted nothing to do with them. We were living parallel lives under the roof of an extremely hostile and unhealthy home environment. As hard as I tried to avoid their influences, it was impossible to prevent their behavior from continuing to drag me down.

Then we moved again, this time to a suburb about an hour away from where I had grown up. My father was going to build my mother's dream house—as he saw it—that would miraculously cure her drinking and allow us all to live happily ever after. It was the summer before my senior year.

It didn't take me long to find the wrong group of people to associate with in my new school. I was seventeen and beginning my senior year with little prospect of graduating on time. The administrator who met with me quickly recognized that I was a work program candidate and placed me in a welding job.

It was 1969, the war in Vietnam was raging on and so were my parents. By the middle of November I had dropped out. The only good that came from that move was that it landed me in the high school that I would eventually return to as a teacher.

$\mathcal{L}$ESSON 3:
$\mathcal{F}$ILLING THE
$\mathcal{E}$MOTIONAL $\mathcal{T}$OOLBOX

$\mathcal{D}$uring my pre-adolescent and teenage years, affecting positive outcomes in my life would have required cognitive and emotional resources I had not yet developed. The idea, for example, that I could transcend my experiences—could pull myself up by my bootstraps—was ridiculous, because I had no boots. I hadn't yet developed the cognitive strategies and emotional management skills to combat my dysfunctional family structure.

I was incapable of overcoming the adversity that surrounded me and hadn't developed the resources that would have given me the "bootstraps" to do so. I was confused, angry and without "bootstraps". That said, I do admit there was no way I was going to pull myself up by my bootstraps even if I would have been capable of doing so. I was way too angry.

My environment, instead of fostering productive coping skills, was rife with incrimination and self-blame. These are two very destructive responses but responses, nonetheless, that are characteristic of stressful environments. All of the negative feelings get channeled toward oneself, and the result is often a growing sense of self-loathing. This kind of internalizing occurs because youth haven't yet learned to communicate their thoughts and feelings about themselves or the situation they're living in to someone outside the family structure.

It's an understatement to say that growing up has always been a difficult process. Under even the best conditions of a nurturing, attentive and functional family a child is still challenged to think positively and feel good about oneself, especially during the tumultuous adolescent years. But it is during those very years that making thoughtful, positive and self-enhancing decisions is vital to our being able to better nurture our potential.

For young people growing up in a setting where there is little or no support there is often nowhere else to turn but inward. It is in this isolating and lonely place of inner thoughts and feelings that youth decide how they are going to understand themselves and how they are going to interact with others. Unfortunately, if driven mostly by confusion and anger, this process leads to a dark and reactionary place.

Consistent guidance, structure, nurturance, realistic expectations, encouragement, involvement, understanding, patience, wisdom and empathy are just some of the elements necessary for young people to have a shot at working toward their potential and ultimate self-actualization.

We are creatures that require nurturance and consistent guidance. We cannot be neglected or abused or abandoned without devastating impacts to our ability to develop healthy and productive coping skills.

$\mathscr{L}$ASTING $\mathscr{I}$MPACTS

$\mathscr{W}$hile growing up my siblings and I rarely, if ever, talked about what we witnessed between our parents, and to this day we still avoid the discussion. There were particular incidents I never discussed with anyone—even my wife. I think I wanted to protect the people I love from visualizing such horrendous acts, and keep them from losing more respect for my mother and father than had already been lost.

But I also believe shame played a huge role in my keeping certain events from my childhood to myself. I was ashamed of my parents, and also myself; feeling as though there were something I could have done to stop the violence sooner, or to have prevented it altogether.

I do remember sitting down with a school counselor once, because I felt as though I just had to talk to someone. I was lost and hurting, and one day in school I found myself pouring my heart out to this man. When I finished his response was effectively: "Well, what do you want me to do about it?" I stood up and walked out.

For an at-risk youth, the challenge of finding someone with whom they can confide in a world where trust is hard to come by can be extremely difficult. Even many adults have difficulty expressing their thoughts and feelings with someone they trust. Positive, sympathetic and supportive role models are not always available—especially for at-risk youth who have already worked hard to alienate themselves from the mainstream.

Perhaps my school guidance counselor was experiencing personal challenges of his own—challenges he was unable or unwilling to tap into in order to establish a productive and compassionate dialogue with me. Perhaps he felt ill-equipped to address the gravity of the problems I had brought to him that day. Perhaps he was simply not a fit candidate for his chosen career. But either way, his dismissal of me that day was another event in my life that I would call upon as I grew more inspired to teach.

Even today, recalling the violence of my childhood also recalls the intensity of emotions that were so prevalent back then. I can feel my heart rate increasing and my breathing becoming more labored. The emotional impact that early childhood traumas can have on us, even into our adult years, is amazing. That is why the cognitive strategies that facilitate emotional management and positive decision making are so important to understand, because they allow us to assume greater responsibility for our thoughts, emotions and behaviors.

A Long, Winding Road

Almost a year after I made my decision to drop out of school, I was home helping my father ice a swollen jaw, after a bar room brawl that he had begun and I'd gotten drawn into. Later that night, two of my closest friends introduced me to my future wife—Jeanne. She and I had heard of each other over the years and my friends had decided it was time for us to meet.

It was love first sight—for me anyway. She on the other hand was quite cautious, given my reputation. I knew I had a lot of work to do. One thing that didn't take me long to realize was that she deserved more than to be hanging around with a high school drop-out.

We became friends, and then began dating. The year and a half that followed was filled with some really wild and fun times, but they were also dangerous and tumultuous. Ultimately I learned the importance of returning to school. Following another reconciliation between my father and I, he offered to help me with the financial aid I needed in order to prepare for the GED exam. I passed by the skin of my teeth.

I'll never forget the day that letter arrived. My parents were equally stressed, so when the letter came from the Cook County Department of Education they opened it first. They were almost as invested in my efforts as I was. I was living at home again and planning to enroll in the local community college. When they read I had been awarded my GED, they called me downstairs and handed me the opened letter. This was one of the happiest and most proud moments of my life. It was a major milestone, which paved the way toward my pursuit of a college education.

I couldn't wait to tell Jeanne, as she too was so instrumental in my success. With her continued support and encouragement I began my college career—two years at the local community college followed by full time upper-level study that earned me a Bachelor of Arts Degree, with a double major in Sociology and Speech & Performing Arts. During this time I also married the love of my life.

Earning my college degree gave me the opportunity for an entry-level position with a commercial real estate developer. My father made the necessary introduction, and I successfully completed the interview process and worked hard to learn the business. After later moving to another firm I rose through the ranks. In nine years I became a window-office guy and Assistant Vice President of the company.

Having earned my stripes, the president of that company asked me to join him as Vice President of a startup company, representing a major insurance company in the liquidation of an extensive portfolio of land holdings. After another five years we'd met all of our business plan objectives and I'd saved enough to change careers, thus fulfilling my promise to one day become a teacher. I went back to college to earn my teaching credentials and began my second career.

⟵⟶

As an adult, I eventually began taking stock of myself and recognizing my own innate abilities. Although I had built a successful career in the private sector, I had this recurring vision of becoming a teacher; and ultimately was fortunate enough to finally be offered the extraordinary opportunity to do so.

Before I left my work in real estate I would often sit in the office of one of my business partners and discuss my growing interest in changing careers—doing something I believed would be more meaningful. Though she thought it odd that I would want to leave a successful career, she affirmed my belief that I would be an effective educator. I would mention this to Jeanne as well, who was always very supportive in encouraging me to follow my heart.

Most of us battle uncertainties about who we are and what we are capable of achieving. It is natural to second guess ourselves, especially when we are uncertain where a challenge may lead us, and I believe most of these uncertainties are rooted in two very powerful and negative emotions: the feelings of fear and failure. In my case I needed to accept the possibility that I could find greater professional value.

There are invaluable lessons to be learned from overcoming fear and failure. If we avoid those challenges we run the risk of not reaching our potential, or never fulfilling a passion, or always struggling to find happiness. We risk spending our whole lives believing that we lack the power to build the lives we want for ourselves, ultimately succumbing to feelings of blame and victimization; and who really wants any of that?

$\mathscr{L}$ ESSON 4:
$\mathscr{R}$ EDEFINING '$\mathscr{V}$ ICTIM'

$\mathcal{O}$ ne of my teaching strategies is to ask students if they would really be proud to stand up and claim that their failures are because of their parents. I stand in the front of the classroom and tell my students to imagine I am a guest speaker, and I am in front of them to confess that well into my adult life I am still a failure because of my parents. Students have commented on how pathetic that would be.

Doing this facilitates a powerful moment, allowing me to then ask: when does this behavior become pathetic? If it is pathetic for an adult in their fifties, is it also pathetic at forty, or thirty? Is it okay to be the victim in your twenties, still placing blame on others and feeling sorry for yourself? Is it okay to be a victim right now, while still in high school? If my students can recognize the senselessness mindset that creates the victim, then they can recognize the power they give away by blaming others.

Wouldn't it be preferable to say, instead: "I am a success despite the challenges posed by those around me"?

This is an example of the kind of experiential instruction that I find is meaningful in the classroom, even though some students may hate hearing it. Many of my students intuitively know that what I'm saying is true, but they are not ready to change yet. They are not ready to give up the idea that they are the victim because they know that if they do they must also change their behavior and they are not willing to do that yet either.

As difficult as it was to accept, I eventually realized that the confusion and anger of my childhood only advanced my belief that I was a victim. Not only did I believe I was a victim, I also believed I didn't have any power to change that. As a kid I knew how other kids lived, and I couldn't help but compare their lives to my own—to imagine being part of another family. It is true that while growing up I couldn't change the course that my family had set, but what I could control was my ability to utilize both strength and wisdom to redefine my experiences.

Redefining my life was a process fraught with challenges, and unfortunately facing these challenges would not come until after I had grown up. Over the course of many years I began to realize my potential by redeveloping a set of core beliefs about myself and the world around me. I determined that the only way I was ever going to get to where I wanted to be was by not allowing the adversity in my life to become a source of weakness. Instead of choosing to be a victim all my life, I found ways to use my adversity as a source of strength.

I got to where I am today—a place of strength and self-fulfillment, in a career that I love—by utilizing the lessons to be found in all of my experiences, even the ugly ones. I made a series of life changing decisions that addressed one overreaching and fundamental aspect of my formative years: that I could choose what my experiences of adversity were going to mean to me. I decided not to live my life as a victim.

I thought through some critical realities, ultimately accepting the challenge of deciding how I was going to most effectively frame my experiences. Only I could decide how to define my experiences, what meaning to ascribe to them and ultimately, how I was going to tap into my past experiences moving forward. This is the framework: about oneself, about lived experiences and about the world, which I often focus on when working with my students. They also have the power to define their experiences. They must decide how to frame their experiences, and determine where those experiences are going to take them. They too have to decide not to live their lives as victims.

But how does a young person best go about doing this? After all, our past experiences, especially the difficult ones, have intense and sometimes conflicting emotions associated with them. For me, those emotions include isolation, shame, embarrassment, blame, confusion and anger. These are the emotional memories that inform who I am in my classroom, as I help students who are trying to address some of their own issues. Many of them are experiencing the same emotional turmoil that I endured growing up, because their family structures are as fractured as mine were. So again, the question remains: *how does an at-risk young person best transcend the inclination towards victimhood, while simultaneously developing effective emotional and behavioral management skills?*

In my own life I've found the teachings of particular psychologists and other professionals extremely useful. The psychologist Dr. Albert Ellis, for example, developed a cognitive model of *Rational Emotive Behavior Therapy* and *Rational Emotive Behavior Education*, during and after his doctoral work at Columbia University. Ellis's model is designed to help others identify when their thoughts are based on irrational beliefs, and to work towards replacing those irrational beliefs with more rational ways of thinking.

Others, like the Assistant Director of the Chicago Institute for Rational Emotive Behavior Therapy, Terry London, have expounded upon the work of Dr. Ellis. As London—a teacher and great influence of mine—has taught me over the years, when we take on the role of a victim we understand ourselves as a helpless recipient of life events. Then we use that framework as an excuse to continue self-defeating patterns of behavior. Ellis identified this excuse making construct as *victimology*. This is one of the obstacles we have to overcome before we're able to improve upon our decision making: the tendency to see events from the perspective of a victim.

It seems that one of the most common irrational beliefs is that everything is someone else's fault. This belief system is powerful and also dangerous—fueling the inclination for excuse making, which then only serves to generate even more irrational beliefs and self-defeating behaviors. The belief that one is simply a victim of one's circumstance is the foundation for a life of dysfunction, and it is based on a thought process that discounts the power of our innate abilities.

Much of this has to do with the way we communicate internally with ourselves—or *self-talk*. Ellis conceptualized the theory that understanding the connection between beliefs, self-talk, and emotional responses is the key to emotional management. The cornerstone of his work is the recognition that it is not what happens to us that creates our emotional responses, but rather it is what we tell ourselves *about* the things that happen that causes our emotional responses.

The difficulty in accepting this approach is that it flies in the face of a commonly socialized belief that it is the stuff that happens *to* us that causes our emotional responses. Though this could not be further from the truth it is what we have been taught to believe: that it is the *event* that causes our emotions rather than our *thinking* about the event.

The result of this kind of thinking is that we become emotional victims to life's events. As Ellis concluded, we have become a *nation of victims* by largely blaming others for how we feel. It's almost as though we wake up in the morning and become a pinball, dropping ourselves into the pinball machine of life and bouncing off the bumpers of things that happen, all day long. No wonder we can become so exhausted, frustrated, confused and angry.

But it doesn't have to be this way. A more productive way of living involves taking responsibility for our thoughts and emotions and their resulting behaviors.

As I begin each school year I challenge my students to break this cycle of destructive thinking and to re-direct their behaviors from self-defeating to self-enhancing. Life is full of choices. Each day we are given the opportunity to make positive decisions, or we can *choose* to make self-defeating decisions. One key to success or failure is the ability to understand and then accept that you have the freedom to *choose* how you want to live your life!

So the question remains: *how do you want to live your life?* Do you want to live it making excuses for your failings by blaming other people? Do you want to live the life of a victim, or do you want to take charge of your decisions?

$\mathcal{D}$ R O P - $\mathcal{O}$ U T T O $\mathcal{T}$ E A C H E R

$\mathcal{W}$hen I returned to the scene of the crime—returned as a teacher, to the high school I'd walked out of in the November of my senior year—I was ready to save all the students in my charge. I believed I had all the answers to their problems. After everything I had been through I believed I had the power to change their lives. While I believed there was potential to achieve this lofty ambition, I didn't realize that it was going to take more than my ambition alone to make any of it happen. It took me a long time to realize that my experience, education and good intentions were not going to allow me to achieve these goals as quickly as I thought.

For a long time I was reluctant to discuss my personal history with my students. That was a mistake. It was a mistake because my struggles are also my strengths, and I want my students to realize that their struggles can be a source of strength for them too. The alternative is that their struggles become a source of weakness, as they did for me, until I had my first epiphany about how I was living my life and why I was living it the way I was.

In my early years of teaching I was concerned about telling my students that I had dropped out of high school—*their* high school, no less—because I was afraid that it might send the wrong message. I feared sending them the message that if I could drop out and still become a teacher then *they* could drop out and still be okay as well. Over time I realized that how I presented my past experiences to my students was just as important as what those experiences were.

Although the challenges and mistakes of my past are not sources of pride for me, I did eventually realize that they were the very experiences that brought me before a group of at-risk high school students, as a teacher who could help make a real difference in their lives. I realized that the adversity I'd faced was what gave me insights inside the classroom. I realized that I had to share my experiences more openly, because doing so set me apart from many of the other teachers these students knew.

I became comfortable discussing my own experiences and failures, and in doing so facilitated the connection these students needed to make with me. Without that connection I would be just another teacher in a long line of teachers who had little or no positive impact. I certainly was not going to be a teacher who distanced himself from these students, assuming that they were too damaged and beyond assistance.

In order to help my students to truly listen to, and then incorporate into their lives, the lessons I want to teach them, I have to be very honest about where I come from and how I got to where I am in my life. I have to be relatable. Without being open and empathetic it is nearly impossible to bridge the gap in the student-teacher relationship. I want to break down the social and institutional barriers that create such gaps.

For example, one afternoon in my classroom I was sharing a personal story in order to better illustrate our point of discussion, when one student asked if other teachers in the high school liked me. Although taken aback by the forthrightness of her question, I knew why she had asked it. I still asked her what had prompted her question and she said "because you do so much to help your students."

I hoped that she and the class would appreciate my answer. I wanted them to realize that we all have our own unique abilities and strengths to offer, and that in this particular case my teaching assignments and the Resource Program[1] I facilitate afford me the interpersonal connections that most teachers don't have the time for. My teaching position is unique compared to that of a mainstream teacher, and so is the fact that I am empathetic to the

---

[1] The Resource Program I teach in has been designed as a support program for students who may still be able to manage the daily demands of a carefully balanced schedule of regular education classes, with only limited special educational classes. Class selection can be as diverse as these young people are. They come from all walks of life. As I have come to realize, dysfunction knows no economic barrier.

While overall behavioral issues lead to eligibility due to various causal factors, I contend that behaviors alone are not the issue that we as educators, parents, social workers and psychologists must address. Behavior is a manifestation of the underlying thought process that leads to the unwelcome behavior and that is what must be addressed. It is the student's internal monologue that we have to focus on, in addition to implementing more tangible changes like altering the student's academic schedule or offering special staff support.

motivations for dropping out of high school, while many of my students are at risk of making the same mistake.

I have the unique position of being able to use my experiences to help guide these young people toward more fulfilling decision making and lifestyle choices. I help problem solve and teach emotional management skills to my students, which aid them in their lives both in and out of school. If I can't help directly, I try to find someone who can.

I went on to tell the class that there were probably other teachers who didn't like me, but that that was okay. There are also plenty of educators who do recognize each other's abilities to make positive impacts in the lives of their students. But not everyone is going to be liked all the time, and we can't expect everyone to like us. I added that all any of us can do is follow our conscience and our passion, and do our best for others as we would want them to do for us. I mentioned that each of us owes it to ourselves to live authentically, and with positive effort things generally work out for the best.

This conversation presented the opportunity for a teaching moment, in which I addressed one cornerstone of emotional management and decision making—the theory that establishes the importance of distancing ourselves from what others may think about us when their thoughts are negative, unhelpful and ill informed.

People—and young people especially—too often allow their egos to get involved in how they relate to others, and sometimes personal insecurities result in our projecting certain ideas, perceptions and judgments onto others. This is a common element in even the most basic social interactions.

Finally, I told my students that what people may think about them is not their problem and that we ought not to take ownership of it. Ignore it. I told them that each of us has to decide how to be true to ourselves in order to have the best opportunities to reach our potential. I want my students to strive for fulfillment in their lives, regardless of how others may misunderstand them.

I often offer a strategy that others understand on an intellectual level but may have difficulty understanding on an emotional level: I suggest that sometimes we have to develop our own encouraging "self-talk", no matter how blunt it may be; for example "it's not humanly possible for me to care any less about what another person thinks or feels about me".

Students often have a hard time with this philosophical approach. It is, however, an effective way of managing our responses to the behavior of others, and also our feelings about any interpersonal conflicts we may have. It is easy to lose a balanced perception of events when we assign too much meaning to the negative thoughts, beliefs and behaviors of others.

Another step towards emotional management and more productive living is having the ability to distance ourselves from negative or unhealthy people. It is essential to guard ourselves against the negative influences of people who either don't know us, or aren't invested in our personal wellbeing.

While we certainly can't control the behavior of other people, we can manage the way we react to their behavior. It is our responsibility to ourselves to not allow the behaviors of others to drag us down. This can be especially true when we are striving to achieve what others are afraid to attempt. I have had many discussions with my students on self-acceptance in the face of criticism, and on having the ability to liberate oneself from negative influences.

It is a powerful quality one can possess: to live confidently in whom you are and what it is that you are trying to achieve. One of the most powerful emotional tools we have is the ability to stay confident in the direction we have set for ourselves and in the knowledge that we are living authentically.

Once, when I was feeling insecure about how to move forward with a group of students, a senior colleague shared his philosophy: he told me to do what I thought would be in the students' best interest and have faith that everything else would be okay. I try to live up to that each day. When my student questioned me about how I manage my feelings about others' opinions of me, I knew I was succeeding.

It is professional moments like this that create very personal moments for me: when I am among these students and we are relating at a level they rarely experience with other adults. My students and I share a mutual understanding about the relatedness of our experiences. This understanding gives me the best chance to make positive impacts in the lives of my students; it is making that all-important interpersonal connection. Let's face it, students rarely, if ever, learn from teachers they don't like or can't relate to.

$\mathcal{B}$ALANCING $\mathcal{A}$CT

$\mathcal{W}$hile teaching offers me tremendous opportunities to positively impact the lives of my students, it also poses an incredible responsibility. Teaching requires that I strike an effective balance between preventing our open communication from breaking down, while at the same time—particularly as a state-mandated reporter—keeping in mind the long-term best interests of my students.

For example, one day a student revealed that she had been getting high with her mother since fifth grade; in another class discussion several students reported getting high with the parents of friends. Today's high school classrooms are filled with students who are struggling through myriad issues such as these, and when discussing such emotional issues—especially those that students have kept bottled up for a long time—communication can break down very easily.

As an educator I need to know when to move forward while discussing a sensitive issue, and when to pull back.

Students will come to class dealing with issues of physical and emotional abuse, or end of life thoughts. Some have experienced hospitalization for depression or rehabilitation from drug dependencies, while others report experiences of molestation or other forms of sexual abuse. These students have endured a wide range of experiences and their feelings about them run deep. This can all get very complicated as a mandated reporter who is obligated to report these types of admissions to social service agencies or, when necessary, to recruit support from our team of school psychologists and social workers.

Another aspect of this balancing act in the dynamics between student and teacher is: *your student must give you permission to become involved in their lives.* That's right: you must be given permission to dig around into someone else's life. Now this doesn't mean that once a student comes to me with an issue they're always going to like how I respond—I still have the responsibility of acting in the best interest of that student, even if they don't always agree with me. But it does mean that I have to wait for students to come to me. They are not going to open the lines of communication because I want or demand that they do. It has to come from them.

Furthermore, that doesn't mean a student will come to me and say: "Hey Mr. Palmer, I've been thinking a lot about you and me and my life and I think you can do wonders with me, so I give you permission to have an impact on me that will start to turn my life around." It doesn't happen that way. But students have the right to give or deny me the permission to try and positively impact their life *because it's their life.*

What I had to learn was that each student, in his or her own way and by their own time table, has to allow me into their lives. Only then will I have a chance to make a positive impact. As I learned to be more patient and became more observant, I could see the process of permission-giving slowly unfold before me. It is a time consuming process, but in order to be effective I have to wait for that moment to arrive.

What I have learned is that to build upon your effectiveness you have to let people know who you are, and in my case, what led me to teaching. I personalize my relationship with my students by carefully and strategically revealing some of the experiences that helped define me. But I avoid getting personal with them.

I bring a level of authenticity to the classroom by tapping into my own *and* their experiences. I can have strong, positive and effective interpersonal relationships with my students without it getting too personal. It also doesn't hurt that I wear my passion for teaching on my sleeve.

There is value in displaying some humanity in the classroom which, in part, can be accomplished by sharing experiences of failure. Why not share that common ground with your students? In today's classroom setting it is crucial to use all our tools to connect with students. If you have a unique experience, use it! When a teacher shares experiences that students can relate to their own lives, it creates greater meaning and purpose to their being in the classroom. It is that kind of connection that enhances learning opportunities.

When I bring real life experiences into the instructional setting—experiences students can directly relate to, it enriches my instruction by giving it more authenticity and greater meaning and purpose. Any effective teacher will tell you that you will never get away with being phony or superficial in the classroom.

Students know sincerity when they see it, and they pick up on it very quickly when you're not. They know when you "get it", they know when a teacher is able to relate to them on a compassionate, empathetic level, and that is a powerful feeling for any young person who is struggling to build a healthy, productive and meaningful life.

$\mathcal{L}$ESSON 5:
$\mathcal{E}$DUCATING $\mathcal{T}$HROUGH $\mathcal{E}$MPATHY

$\mathcal{Y}$oung people know when others "don't get it". One of the worst things an adult can do is fake it; to try and portray themselves as having an authentic understanding of the very personal and private experiences of growing up under challenging circumstances, if they do not in fact, share similar experiences. Such adults, no matter their intentions, risk losing the chance to make a meaningful connection with the young people they're trying to reach.

I believe there is a lack of patience in adults who believe they "get it", or who try to manufacture empathy in an authentic way. Young people shouldn't be met with insincerity, ignorance or impatience.

There are also adults who attempt to utilize their positions of authority to get positive results from young people. That is not going to succeed either. Such misdirected efforts will only further alienate the population they're trying to serve. The key is to know your audience and tailor your interactions with them accordingly. Did you ever have a teacher who didn't seem to have a clue, and worse yet, didn't realize it? That's what I'm talking about.

I advise educators to recognize that the foundation for the behavior of students who grow up in dysfunctional, fractured environments is one of confusion and anger. There is often blame imposed in such environments and tragically, students suffer the most. In such situations transitioning into the classroom, with all of its demands, is often more than a student can successfully manage. Their confusion and anger are further fueled by growing resentment and rebellion, and oftentimes become directed at the teacher, who represents those classroom demands.

Students will even compare their teacher with their parent: measuring the focal point of the classroom against the focal point of family dysfunction. Daily transitions from a dysfunctional family setting into an overwhelming school environment often result in the student shutting down as a defense mechanism. Much of this explains why it can be very challenging when a teacher is faced with an at-risk student.

A long time ago my most valued colleague, mentor and friend taught me the principle: *sometimes you have to do nothing before you can do something.*

Let me illustrate this point by relating a situation that another one of my many mentors faced in his school cafeteria. He was on cafeteria supervision when he saw an upperclassmen sitting on a cafeteria table, talking to a girl, cigarette pack in his shirt pocket, and his baseball hat cocked to one side. He knew he should not being sitting on the table, displaying a pack of cigarettes, and he knew not to wear his hat cocked as this can signify a gang affiliation. In spite of this display, he wasn't necessarily looking for a confrontation. He was just posturing for the benefit of his own ego and perception of self. Basically, he wanted to impress the girl.

As my mentor tells it, he stood across the cafeteria from this student, contemplating the situation and considering his options. He figured there were a couple of ways to handle this situation. He could get the student's attention by yelling across the cafeteria, and then gesture for him to get off the table, lose the cigarettes, and straighten his hat. How effective do you think that would have been? Imagine the hundred or so other students that certainly would have heard him and probably just as many more that would have seen him signaling to this student in an effort to make him comply.

If he had selected that option what do you think his chances of gaining this young man's compliance would have been? Moreover is the question of my mentor's motivation to approach this situation in such a public manner. What would have been *his* motivation? Would it have been to simply gain compliance or to assert authority?

Would a public strategy have been the best strategy, or would it have been a reflection of my mentor's need to demonstrate power and control? Would this have been a response rooted in anger, because he was saying to himself: "This kid is way out of line" and "Who does he think he is, undermining my authority in front of all these students?"

That sort of distorted thinking personalizes behavior. When ego gets involved your judgment becomes compromised. Fortunately, my mentor knew that this student's behavior had nothing to do with him and everything to do with the student. With a sensible and effective way of thinking in place, his ego wasn't interfering with his thought process.

If he hadn't been thinking along those lines he could have very easily acted out this situation publicly, which would have been a mistake. Trying to gain this young man's compliance in a public manner would only serve to embarrass the student and put him in a defensive position, decreasing the likelihood of the student complying. Also, my mentor did not have a relationship with this student. Publicly attracting attention to him would have risked embarrassment-fueled anger and the possibility of a confrontation.

Likely, all of this would have accelerated into a downward spiral of conflict that would have landed the kid in the Dean's office. It would have driven a wedge between the young man and my mentor. It also would have driven a wedge between him and those other students who were witness to what would have been an ego-driven behavior. Equally important, his behavior would have risked driving an institutional wedge between the students and the school as a whole.

What he did was examine three alternatives. The first was to walk over to the student, speak quietly and ask for compliance. The second option was to write him a please and thank you note and discreetly pass it to him as he walked by his table. The third option was to simply avoid the whole situation by ignoring him. Which do you think he chose?

What my mentor actually did was write this student a very short note and passed it to him as he walked by. He then walked to another supervisory post and observed the student for his reaction. The young man took the note and put it in his shirt pocket, and the pack of cigarettes went into his backpack; he then took a seat at the table and fixed his hat. When he looked up, they made eye contact and exchanged a nod. That was it. As he was leaving the cafeteria at the end of the hour, my mentor caught up to the student, quietly and respectfully told him how much he appreciated his decision and thanked him. He also told him that the next time he saw the student with cigarettes, the pack would be confiscated and after that there could be an intervention by the Dean's office. The student appreciated the candor.

This young man felt respected and that was the key. This situation required no ego, no power struggle and no public display of power or authority; just a private interaction between two people with the one in authority showing respect for the one with less power. Success was achieved because there wasn't a misuse of power. In this case less was more.

This point is essential: *power does not always exist just because you think you have it.* It's a misperception to think that exhibiting power is the only way to uphold a position of authority. When working with teenagers, and especially at-risk youth within a school setting, the less power one asserts the more power one actually has.

Young people respect those who conduct themselves in a measured and respectful manner. These young people accept a teacher's ability to exercise power when they trust that teacher not to abuse it. What I hope teachers—and anyone in a position of authority—gain from this example is to realize the impact of true power.

I've had similar encounters with students, and when I assert the least amount of power possible I have the best chance of success. This is the "less is more" practice that builds a bridge between teacher and student, instead of driving a wedge between the two.

It is a student-centered approach that focuses on achieving the most desired outcome, instead of simply asserting power. I succeed in difficult situations by treating young people with the same amount of dignity and respect that I would have wanted someone to treat me with when I was a student. I succeed by tapping into the patience that comes from understanding the situation and the people in it.

$\mathscr{E}$XPECTATIONS & $\mathscr{N}$EGOTIATIONS

$\mathscr{I}$n the cafeteria my mentor created a positive social interaction with this student by being empathic and showing the student respect for whom he was and the situation he was in. When I'm working with teenagers who have been identified as at-risk because of emotional and behavioral disturbances due, in part, to earlier life trauma, it is critical to establish an effective relationship with that student. Developing this relationship can take a long time—but it also took the student a long time to get where they are.

Do you have to be a high school drop out to be meaningful teacher or mentor or parent? Do you have to have come from a dysfunctional family? Do you have to have experienced domestic violence first hand or have witnessed alcohol abuse? Of course not. So what is the key that offers some teachers an advantage in connecting with students? I am convinced that, in part, it is an authentic understanding of your audience, a thoughtful and reflective recognition of their emotional struggles and the ability to leave your ego and expectations at the door.

When we insert our perceived expectations upon others we become less effective at building healthy relationships and meeting our goals. When we insert too much of ourselves—our emotions, motivations, demands or expectations into a situation, we risk failure to achieve the goal of that interaction.

In the instructional setting, if a teacher doesn't have a firm understanding of their student's experiences then that teacher is going to have a hard time finding effective ways to work with at-risk students. As important as it is to make an authentic connection with your students, in or out of the classroom, it is equally important to be mindful of how you negotiate your expectations for your students. This is especially true of at-risk youth because if they sense you have expectations that they will be unable or unwilling to meet, you risk setting them up for failure from the beginning.

What each of us must understand is that our interactions are a process of negotiation and an effective negotiator understands the needs and desires of the people with whom he or she is interacting. If you want to maximize both short and long-term effectiveness in your relationships with others, you must realize this is largely not accomplished by edict. It is not accomplished by autocratic, rigid or dogmatic demands that certain expectations be met simply because they are demanded. What I am describing transcends the "because I said so" shortcut syndrome of teaching—rather it is accomplished through effective communication and negotiation. As a

teacher, this also includes effective classroom management. My classroom management philosophy is: *when
given the right set of circumstances students will work to meet
their teacher's expectations.*

FEAR, FORGIVENESS & CHANGE

When I was fifteen I landed a job at the local gas station (child labor laws were less restrictive back then) where, I'll note, I was allowed to buy cigarettes for my mother. I started that job the summer before my sophomore year and at that time it was the best thing that could have happened to me.

The owner was the hardest working man I have ever met. His best friend was a warm and caring man who had unfortunately become a serious alcohol abuser. These two men had grown up together, but as young men had taken different paths. The owner had built a successful business for himself and was living the American Dream—a family and a house in the suburbs, two cars in the garage. His friend slept on oil crates in the back room of the gas station; he was just grateful to have a roof over his head.

These guys knew my parents and they knew what I was going through. They knew when my mother was hiding her black eyes behind her sunglasses. They knew things were tough when I would just want to hang out with them. They knew things were bad when I would ask for more hours, or when I would make myself available if someone didn't show up for work. They knew my sense of embarrassment and shame when my mother would pull into the gas station, drunk. They knew how much I needed that job and how much I valued working there.

These two men became my anchors. I felt grounded and safe when I was with them. I sought their guidance and I would listen for learning moments. They helped guide me into early manhood by showing me what manhood looked like. In many ways they were shepherding me through two and a half very important years in my life.

The owner's friend would disappear on drinking binges, not showing up to work for days. Then, the owner would end up working double shifts or working twice as hard during the shifts they shared. I would often be called in when this occurred and would witness the frustration and disappointment in the face of the owner as he worried about his friend. What amazed me was that he always accepted his friend back to work when he would return. I know there were many times he just wanted to give up and fire him, but he wouldn't do it. The loyalty of friendship was more important, even though it wasn't always reciprocal.

These two men exemplified what it takes to work through difficult and challenging situations in our lives. They did this together; through the strength of the love and commitment they had for each other even in the face of substance abuse, betrayal and neglected responsibilities at work. The gas station owner knew not to take his friend's weakness and his inability to reconcile his own inner conflicts as a personal affront. He knew his friend was navigating some serious challenges and he was not going to abandon him because he was disappointed or frustrated with him. Those two men remained friends until the end.

As I look back on the years that I worked at that gas station, I realize the parental-type guidance that I benefitted from came to me by the two men who took me under their wings. I was in awe of these two men, who taught me the meaning of friendship and even more about the value of work. They taught me about the importance of loyalty and honesty. They taught me about forgiveness. The owner would not abandon his friend—there was always forgiveness.

ear is a powerful emotion and it plays a pivotal role in both our ability to change and in the practice of forgiveness—forgiveness of ourselves and forgiveness of others. Fear is one of the main reasons we cling to self-defeating behaviors, and struggle to forgive ourselves our failings.

In part we fear that if we change a behavior it will result in other aspects of our life changing in ways that feel uncertain to us. Changing our behaviors may also risk influencing changes in others' expectations of us—another scary prospect for a young person. For example, when a young person realizes the connection between a lack of self-forgiveness and self-defeating behaviors, they may then learn to re-manage their thinking. This, in turn, may enable them to develop new, self-enhancing behaviors.

Many of us can relate to the teacher who becomes so enthusiastic about a student's positive behavior that they lose sight of how difficult it was for the student to make the transition from self-defeating to self-enhancing decision making and behavior. However well-intentioned, for the student this results in an increase in the pressure to maintain that level of performance. This can be an intimidating feeling, and it contributes to a student's unwillingness to change.

Another reason many young people resist change is basic rebellion. This is especially true if one is experiencing anger or resentment—as I did in my youth, and as many at-risk youth do today. So we dig in our heels and refuse to change.

Yet another motivation behind intransigence is a lack of acceptance for who we have become—a rejection of one's own identity. I often ask my students whether they are who they want to be, and most of the time they are not pleased with their sense of identity. Too often, however, youth are displeased with themselves because of a negatively biased assessment of who they are compared to who they believe they should be. Young people can become very unforgiving of themselves when their perceptions are such.

For many people this can be a very deep-seated problem. Some of us really don't understand why our lives are so tangled up in turmoil and conflict. Often this conflict is perpetuated by the adults or other significant people in our lives. Unfortunately, those of us who grew up in dysfunctional homes often believe that *their* behavior—the behavior of those around us—is or was our fault. A young person may also think that if they were only a "better person" or behaved differently that the behavior of the people around them would change too—a false belief.

However, instead of acknowledging that the unhappiness, anger, conflict and dysfunction in their home life is not their responsibility, young people often direct their frustration and anger toward themselves, and this self-blame can become a very destructive force.

This can develop into some very serious self-loathing, and the resulting frustration and anger are directed toward both oneself and others. This is the life of a victim: the tendency to deny one's own power to affect change by becoming consumed with anger and blame. This is yet another cycle of destructive behavior that must be re-managed.

For those who believe that the abuse, which stems from family conflict, is your fault, there is a lot of work to be done to recover. But how do we do this? How do we recover from the adversity that we have been subjected to by the people who are supposed to be closest to us?

The simple truth is that self-forgiveness is integral to moving forward. But anger towards yourself interferes. This anger makes it nearly impossible to address the underlying issues that impact our decisions and behaviors. Two possibilities exist: either you don't believe you deserve self-forgiveness or you intuitively know that if you do forgive yourself, a change in behavior logically follows and you are not willing to do that yet. Of course, it often is a combination of the two concerns. As Dr. Ellis taught, anger is a classic response to feelings of inadequacy and blame. It is, as well, compensatory behavior to mask negative feelings against oneself and the world.

As Ellis would say, you might tell yourself you are an idiot for behaving idiotically—one moment of behavior becomes an all-encompassing overgeneralization and needless label, that only serves to perpetuate our negative self-talk. Ellis believed these kinds of negative labels are a major source of significant emotional disturbance.

There is a way to break this pattern and it starts with recognizing your dislike for yourself and then forgiving yourself. Self-forgiveness allows you to leave the past where it belongs: in the past. This self-forgiveness is really the most effective way to move yourself forward. I believe this is at the heart of more effective emotional management and decision making. However, this can also be really difficult to do.

I was talking about self-forgiveness one day and several students were resisting the whole idea of it. But one young man was particularly troubled over the concept, so later when I had a moment with him I walked him down the hall. I told him to go into the washroom and look at himself in the mirror, make eye contact and to forgive himself for everything by saying "I forgive me for everything". As I suspected he was unwilling—unable really—to do that. He could barely look himself in the eye.

Here was a handsome sixteen year old who took great pride in how he looked. He was always very well groomed and he dressed in the best clothes he could afford. Looking at him, you knew that he spent a lot of time choosing his wardrobe and styling his hair. As is the case with most sixteen year old boys, the way he looked was very important to him. But that day in school he looked at me and said: "Mr. Palmer, I'm afraid I'm not going to be able to do that". He is certainly not alone. Most people struggle to forgive themselves.

We often convince ourselves that self-forgiveness is too simple a solution; that it just can't be that easy to let ourselves off the hook for accidents, poor decisions and mistakes in judgment that we regret. As difficult as it is, we must admit to and then forgive our own faults as readily as we do with the people around us. We forgive other people and do so often, so what is so difficult about forgiving ourselves? Perhaps the answer is just as simple as this: too many of us don't like ourselves as much as we like other people!

So what can you do? You can focus on the fact that almost anyone who cares for you would forgive you your wrongs, and in recognizing this you can tell yourself over and over again: "If another person can forgive me, then I can forgive me." But it will take practice.

LESSON 6: MANAGING SELF-TALK OR, DON'T 'SHOULD' ON YOURSELF AND TRY NOT TO 'MUST'ERBATE

As I discuss the complexities of this challenge with my students I suggest the idea of their gaining power by acknowledging and then harnessing their own abilities. We talk about two essential skills: listening to ourselves and being honest with ourselves. Ellis discussed our internal monologues as *self-talk*. Whatever you choose to call it, it is our tool for processing our thoughts and sorting through all the things that occur in our lives.

When we are immersed in our private thoughts—self-talk—it is crucial to be as candid and objective as possible. We don't really think about our patterns of self-talk much, if at all, but it is the single most dominating force behind all of our emotions and behaviors. One of the keys to understanding our self-talk is to recognize the belief system that informs it.

It is our self-talk that determines our emotional reactions and behavioral responses to life's events. It is our processing tool—informing how we interact with ourselves, others and the world around us. It guides us through our daily experiences and tells us how to behave.

Our self-talk, like our emotions, does not work in isolation. We can't have an emotion without a thought. All of this processing occurs in the prefrontal cortex. If I were to have that part of my brain removed I would no longer have the ability to think, and therefore, emote. As I explain this to my students the connection between thinking and feeling becomes clearer.

We habitually refer to our feelings: I'm feeling good, or I'm feeling lousy; I'm feeling happy, depressed, angry, lonely and so on. The reality is that none of these feelings can occur without the thoughts that precede them. One might ask: *why am I having this feeling?* The simple truth is that it is reflective of the set of core philosophical beliefs that influence our thoughts and cause our emotional responses—philosophical beliefs that are informed by external factors like economic and social class, gender, sexual orientation, race, ethnicity, faith, education and even geography.

Our self-talk bridges the gap between our core philosophy and our emotional responses—a cognitive function that many of us don't give much thought to on a daily basis. This is partly because we are creatures of habit and self-talk is a habitual mechanism. But it is also because our thought processes occur at such a naturally rapid pace, to pause and think about our thinking would require intentionally interrupting that cognitive process—a skill that takes time to develop.

If I were to diagram this cognitive process, it would look something like this:

EXTERNAL ——➤ SELF-TALK ——➤ EMOTIONS ——➤ BEHAVIORS
STIMULUS

So many of my students cling to the notion that it is the external influences of events or other people that are responsible for their own behaviors—a largely socialized way of thinking. These teenagers will find any excuse to insist that they are not responsible for their own behaviors. They often reject the solutions to their emotional and self-defeating decision making in order to hold on to this belief. They are stubborn in their insistence that it is always someone else's fault.

There is often real fear in changing this habit, and many of us are reticent to openly acknowledge our efforts to change the way we are thinking and living because of a fear of failure. It is bad enough if we don't succeed, but if others are also aware that we have tried and failed, it is often too much for many of us. This is especially true with adolescents.

I'm reminded of one of my most able students whose talents and skills were frequently eclipsed by her intransigence. When she was placed in my Resource Program[2]

---

[2] See footnote 1, page 64

she was desperate. She had been in trouble with the local police for vandalism and her relationship with her parents had deteriorated to the point where effective, positive communication was nonexistent. Her academics were suffering, she was socially isolated and she had an extremely low sense of self-worth.

But she was also very capable and she wanted to achieve greater success. In spite of the difficulties within her family structure, her parents wanted to be more supportive. She also knew that the Resource Program was where she needed to be if she was going to turn things around; and she did. After graduating from high school she went on to graduate from college with a degree in Special Education and is now teaching at-risk elementary school students.

She was in the Resource Program for three years and during that time she would insist that it was the event (whatever that happened to be) that was responsible for her emotional reactions, not her beliefs about the event. She was incredibly consistent in holding on to her expressed beliefs. It wasn't until the last day of her senior year that she finally relented and confessed that she had realized long before that she was in charge of her reactions, but that she didn't want to give in to what I had been teaching... like I didn't already know that.

The truth of the matter is that she had quietly accepted responsibility for her emotions and had become remarkably successful at managing them. Without that skill she would not have achieved the success she had in high school and later, in college. I see this unfold often when students are trying to decide whether they are going to buy into what I am communicating.

Most start out believing that they have no other choice but to cling to their expressed beliefs, because to accept the principle that individually they are each responsible for the way they react to life events seems threatening. The reason this is so threatening is because by accepting responsibility for their behaviors, they no longer have someone or something to blame—*they will be forced to let go of their identity as a victim, in favor of a new one.*

Making this change requires a major paradigm shift, and although this particular student was working through the process that would enable her to begin accepting more responsibility for her emotions, she was not yet ready to openly express that she was moving in that direction. She saw it as too risky. Instead she privately made the cognitive shift so she would not be seen as having failed if her efforts were unsuccessful.

Ultimately however, she was successful. On the last day of her senior year she presented me with a gift which is prominently displayed in my home. It is a plaque which, in part, reads:

"IT'S NOT THE EVENT
IT'S THE WAY YOU REACT TO THE EVENT"
OUTSTANDING TEACHER AWARD

Mr. Palmer

This young woman was not very different from most of the young people I teach. Students are a reflection of society's socialization process, just as you and I are. Unfortunately, some of us are socialized to believe in the dominant force of external events, which then allows us to place blame outside ourselves. We learn this very young and it quickly becomes habit.

Personal empowerment is one of my main focuses when trying to help students realize that they can transcend environmental circumstances by re-conditioning themselves to engage in more self-enhancing and productive ways of thinking and behaving. At the most basic level my message is rooted in understanding that the thought processes create emotions which result in behavior. It is always in this order.

THOUGHTS
create
EMOTIONS
that result in
BEHAVIORS

Understanding this process is everyone's best chance at changing ineffective and self-defeating patterns of thinking and behaving. I also refer to this cognitive shift as *cognitive restructuring* because it seeks to fundamentally restructure the way we think, and therefore, the way we perceive ourselves, others and world conditions.

As you practice listening to your self-talk, start by trying to evaluate whether you are demanding that something should or must occur. Then try to identify whether you are converting what is only a preference or a desire into a need. Ellis concluded that when we convert a *preference* into an *absolute necessity* and don't get what we believe we need, we upset ourselves.

Dr. Ellis amusingly coined the term: *"must"urbation*—the habit of making a demand on ourselves, others or on the world and feeling entitled to that demand being met. This kind of thinking can become deeply engrained in our belief system. People believe their demands are reasonable and that others and the world around them *should* or *must* meet their demands.

Dr. Ellis's contention was that "must"urbation is based on demands, plus three other irrational beliefs and habits: *awfulizing* (the perception of dread), *low frustration tolerance* (impatience), and *labeling and damning* (toward self, others, and/or world conditions). Ellis concluded that if you have one of these irrationalities you most likely suffer from all three.

Demandingness is based on the notion that you must get whatever it is that you are demanding because it is your belief that things must be the way you demand. It is also based on the distorted belief that you are right and the world is wrong. It is a by-product of an ego disturbance that is rooted in a sense of self-righteousness caused by an inflated ego.

Awfulizing is a powerful emotional force that causes significant upset. People who awfulize life's realities view their experience or the experiences of others' from the perspective that life's circumstances are awful, horrible and terrible. Ellis also refers to this extreme version of awfulizing as *catastrophizing*, in other words, viewing life circumstances as *catastrophic.*

These are negative and irrational ways of understanding the world, and only serve to fuel unhealthy and unproductive emotions. For the person who awfulizes, the simplest setbacks can become the source of significant emotional turmoil. An unpleasant event in their life becomes unbearable and *should* never have happened. At the root of awfulizing is a fundamental sense of anxiety, worry or dread brought on by the irrational belief that events must be the way we *demand* they *should* be. Ellis remarks that irrational beliefs also result in people *should* *"ing"* on themselves, and others as well.

People who experience *low frustration tolerance* suffer from the belief that life is so difficult or terrible that they can't bear it. I frequently see this in students, as they become increasingly intolerant over an unmet demand for immediate feedback, reinforcement or gratification.

The last category of Ellis's theory of "must"urbation is *labeling and damning*. This involves making "I" and "You" statements that are almost always the result of errant overgeneralizations. A few examples would be self-talk statements like: "I can't believe I did that, I must be an absolute idiot" or "I hate myself".

What happens next is a rapid succession of negative, self-defeating thoughts, which are then reinforced by consistent recurrences of the same. Ellis came to the conclusion that rehearsing negative thoughts intensifies negative emotions, and that "must"urbation becomes a habitual process that is very difficult to overcome.

When demands for ourselves, others or the world around us go unsatisfied we will invariably become upset. In other words, when we believe that things *should* be a certain way or that our way is the way things *must* be, and our expectations go unrealized, we will upset ourselves. When we convert a preference into an absolute necessity, or a "must" belief, convincing ourselves that we have to have what we believe we need, and don't experience our demanded outcome, we inevitably experience emotional upset.

Ellis would say that our absolute needs are for food, water and shelter. The rest are simply desires or preferences. Maintaining perspective and recognizing that just because you want something to be a certain way does not mean that it must be that way is the first step to re-managing this kind of self-talk.

⌒

But how do we get in touch with our self-talk? As you are reading these words, do you catch yourself in moments of internal monologue? For example, you may be thinking: "what is this guy talking about?" or "don't tell me it's what I'm thinking that causes my reactions, because it's the stuff that happens to me that causes my reactions!" That is your inner voice doing what all of our inner voices do, and it is this inner voice that we engage before making any decisions. It is our *self-talk*.

Dr. Ellis developed a formula called the "ABC" model, to which he later added D and E. When understood and put into daily practice, this formula will lead to greater emotional stability, more content and controlled living and greater meaning and purpose:

"A" = Activating Event
(Stuff that happens)

"B" = Belief System
(Stuff you tell yourself based on your beliefs or core philosophy)

"C" = Consequence
(Emotional Consequence: how we react)

"D" = Disputation
(Analysis of the irrational beliefs)

"E" = Effective new ways of thinking, emoting and behaving

Listed below are some examples of negative self-talk—things that most of us have probably said to ourselves at one time or another. As you read the list honestly, many of these statements will probably sound familiar.

They fall under "B"—Belief Systems, because our self-talk directly reflects our beliefs:

"B" – Belief Systems
I can't believe it…
How could this happen…
Why does this happen to me…
Life just isn't fair...
This sucks...
This shouldn't happen...
I can't stand this...
This is stupid...
That person is a jerk; I shouldn't have to listen...
I'll do it later...
I don't care anymore...
So what if I fail...
Screw it; it just doesn't matter...
So what, it's not like I care anyway...
My parents don't care so why should I…

I never get any recognition when I do well, so why try...
I can never do anything right...
I am never going to need to know this...
I just want to quit doing everything...
It's too hard...
Nothing I do matters anyway...
I hate my life...
That person hates me...
It's not my fault...
I'm a loser...
If only I had it to do over again...
I'm no good...
If I wasn't such a rotten person, bad things wouldn't happen...
You can't talk to me like that...
After all I've done for them...
I must do well...
I'm worthless...
People must treat me fairly...
They must live up to my expectations...
This can't happen...
What will people think of me...
I need to be liked...
I'll show them and they'll be sorry...
It's awful....horrible....terrible...
It won't make a difference; why even try...

All of us have engaged in many of these self-talk statements, and oftentimes they are due to a low sense of personal value, exacerbated by low frustration tolerance, ego anxiety, discomfort disturbance or anger. This habit of feeling badly about yourself, along with the people and the world around you, takes a long time to develop. It also takes a lot of practice to get good at these self-defeating thoughts. When we have mastered this pattern of thinking we have also resigned ourselves to a life of self-defeating emotions and behaviors.

All the work that we do to get in the way of our own happiness and success causes us to develop patterns of thoughts, emotions and behaviors that are very difficult to reverse. In order to do so we first have to recognize that this is what we have been doing. Only then can we start the process of becoming happier and healthier people capable of living more authentic, meaningful and purposeful lives.

⟆

In psychological terms, the habit of blaming external events for our self-talk and resulting behaviors is called having an *external locus* of control. You can take control of your emotional reactions to life's activating events, but you must first believe that only you control your cognitive process. When you do, you move from this external locus of control to an *internal locus* of control— putting yourself in charge and further enabling you to become more pro-active. To do this takes a lot of practice and you have to be prepared to fully commit yourself to the effort.

The best way to move forward is to accept the premise that it is our own unique set of beliefs about ourselves, others and the world around us that establishes the nature of our self-talk. To move forward we must accept that our belief system directly affects our thoughts, emotions, and behaviors.

$\mathcal{B}$EING $\mathcal{L}$ABELED

$\mathcal{A}$t one of our high school's institute days I re-counted to a group of my colleagues what had happened to me as a teenager, after a label was hung around my neck. It was at a time when support services in one's home school did not exist, so the idea of challenging a student's beliefs and thought processes in an effort to modify behavior was not available as part of a home school program or curriculum.

But labeling was what we did back in the day too, albeit without the analysis we see today. Unlike today, it was based on IQ testing and achievement. There were no emotional or social analyses done. Unfortunately, IQ tests alone can be highly suspect and certainly should not be used as the single measurement of one's ability. There are simply too many variables that affect the outcome of IQ testing. For example, being up half the night listening to parents fighting!

My colleagues and I were having a discussion about the impact of labeling and mislabeling, when I mentioned that

I was mislabeled in high school and had been "grouped" and "tracked". Back then the high school counselor and administrators responsible for examining IQ test scores took a look at mine, alongside my record of academic achievement prior to high school. They determined that I was going nowhere academically and enrolled me in what would be considered a non-academic, trade school path.

The result was that I was placed in all the shop classes in my sophomore year. I was enrolled in Auto, Woods and Metal shop classes and later, a work program where I was to learn the basics of arc/stick and oxy-acetylene/gas welding. I was labeled, grouped and tracked into a program that was considered to be in my best interest, but in reality may not have been.

As I understand it, this placement decision was simply an expedient solution to my low academic achievement, which sent me into the backwaters of the high school educational environment. The consequence was that the label followed me until the day I dropped out.

$\mathcal{L}$ESSON 7:
$\mathcal{S}$OCIETY'S $\mathcal{N}$EED TO
$\mathcal{L}$ABEL

$\mathcal{I}$ once tried to explain the nature of the student population that I teach to my then-elderly father—attempting to explain the difference between a reluctant learner and a recalcitrant learner. All he understood was that I teach the "bad students". I said: "Dad, imagine two donkeys. The donkey that stubbornly stands in front of you as you tug on the reins is the reluctant learner. The donkey who decides to sit down as you tug on the reins is the recalcitrant learner". This analogy was still completely lost on Dad. As far as he was concerned, I still taught the "bad students".

The simple truth is that most of the students I teach are talented and intelligent, but their potential has been seriously challenged by their low sense of self. These young people have been identified by teachers, counselors, administrators and/or health care professionals as being at-risk. Diagnosticians, social workers and school psychologists have identified them with a Behavior/Emotional Disorder. These are two of the more disturbing labels with which we burden young people. For many years the designation of Behavior Disorder was one that I was able to manipulate in working with students who were labeled as such. I would tell them that it was my opinion BD stood for "Bad Decisions" but that it could also stand for "Better Decisions".

I hold a Master of Arts in Educating Students with Behavior Disorders. I have also accumulated over fifty post-graduate hours of study in the area of emotional management. The funny thing is, from a philosophical perspective I'm not sure I fully comprehend what it means when we talk about behavior disorders. That said, clearly society has certain beliefs about what behaviors are within "normal" standards. Within the field of education and educational psychology we have developed a wide range of testing instruments that are supposed to reflect such expectations and standards.

I dislike labels. My issue is that just because someone does not comfortably fit within a certain standard or expectation does not necessarily mean that person has a behavior disorder. From a sociological perspective I understand how we become uncomfortable when one's behavior does not fit the "norm", so to satisfy our comfort zone we have to find an explanation. We search for meaning by trying to define the behavior. In other words, we feel the need to call it something. We think if we can give it a name, we will know how to manage it.

We label in order to categorize behaviors that lead to underachievement, or behaviors that are otherwise non-compliant. We are more comfortable if we are able to identify someone's behaviors as one thing or another. We believe that if we can name it, we can explain it. The label offers us a structure which we believe gives us a better understanding of what is going on. In a way we are able to understand it better if we can come up with a "diagnosis" and a "label".

These young people whom we label are struggling with myriad issues. They know they are underachieving. They know they have been placed in a special program. They have sat in meetings where the outcomes of their achievement, intelligence and social-emotional testing are discussed. These young people listen to all the issues and concerns and then they hear the labels being assigned and the placement recommendations that are made. They sit there absorbing these attacks to their sense of self. Then they get placed in a program with intervention strategies[3].

---

[3] We have a new state mandated program called Response to Intervention (RtI), designed to intervene within the regular education setting after identifying a student who is failing or at risk of failing. The design is one of collaboration and support in an effort to prevent failure and/or a special education placement. My fear is that this will only facilitate a watered-down curriculum and a move towards "teaching the test" in an effort to avoid the time and work involved in the collaboration process.

We also implement a lengthy document called an Individualized Educational Program (IEP) that becomes the guiding document for a student's education. It includes several goals and objections that are supposed to be adhered to and tracked for accuracy and progress, in the hopes of improving a student's behavior and achievement.

It can be an awkward and uncomfortable process when a group of authority figures are meeting about a student's academic and behavioral issues, when the subject of the meeting is also sitting at the table. I will frequently try to soften the emotional blows to the student's sense of value through positive body language—a well-timed smile or a nod indicating that things are going to be okay—but it can still be a difficult situation for everyone.

In these settings a Special Service's administrator coordinates the meeting, a diagnostician, a school psychologist and a social worker, all of whom report on ability, achievement, and social and emotional testing. There is also a speech and language pathologist who reports on any expressive or receptive language issues, the school nurse who reports on the results of vision and hearing tests and who also records any medications the student is taking at home and that the health office might need to administer during the school day such as attentional, anti-depressant, and/or anti-anxiety drugs. The parent or guardian is also in attendance. Then there is myself: the Program Manager[4]—the person responsible for monitoring the student's progress.

Imagine how the dynamics of this meeting impact a young person's sense of self. This student already knows he or she has been struggling in school. They are also likely struggling with familial relationships and are probably not making the best decisions within their peer group either. The discussion often focuses on how poorly the student is performing in school and some educated guesses as to why that may be, all while the subject of the meeting is sitting right there.

---

[4] See footnote 1, page 64.

Try and place yourself in those shoes. The short and long term effects on oneself are potentially enormous. After all, the student has known for longer than anyone else that things aren't right. They know they have been failing. They know they have been feeling lost, or lonely, or frustrated, or insecure; and they know they have been making decisions that are not in their best interest.

No one has to tell them they are discouraged or angry. No one has to tell them they are experiencing social or familial struggles. No one has to tell them that going to school every day is like being thrown into a meat grinder. They have hated school for as long as they can remember and worse, have hated themselves. *They know.*

Now, consider the parent's anger and frustration. That is when things can become even more difficult. When a parent is overly emotional, when there is a lot of anger toward their teen, or between the parents, or at the school, the situation can become heated. The dynamics vary from blame, to incriminations, to recriminations and even threats. There can be yelling and crying and a lot of personal family issues exposed.

Imagine the thoughts and emotions this teenager comes away with. This is where I try to pick up the pieces. With a special education placement confirmed: eligibility approved and a label assigned, I will often take the student to my classroom to decompress and build a new academic schedule[5]. My goal at this critical juncture is to provide the student a sense of ownership over what is happening; we

---

[5] A new schedule is often necessary when special education courses replace regular education courses, or when low-average replaces average courses within the regular education setting, and/or when a Resource class with me is added.

are partnering to come up with a plan and a new schedule. It helps to mitigate the damage when I include the student in the decision making process, creating the sense that the student is valued and has input in the changes being made.

Making the transition in the midst of a school term can be difficult for a student. It is often daunting to be introduced to new teachers and a new class—especially a special education class—mid-semester. What I try to bring to the mix is the culmination of my own struggles as a student, being as reflective and empathic as I can be, to help the student believe he or she is not alone. Not all students are eager participants at this point, and this is where the challenge continues.

For example, one young man was placed in my Resource class during a meeting I was not in attendance for and he was really pissed-off about it, in part because his open period was being taken away. But he was also angry because his alcohol-abusing mother was part of the decision making process and their relationship was volatile. So he especially didn't want anything to do with the placement decision. I happened to be in the hall outside the Special Services office when he stormed out of the meeting. I was having a conversation with one of the Deans who happened to know the young man and who then went on to tell me a bit about his anger issues and his mother's drinking.

Part of the policy stated that if this student wasn't in attendance for my Resource class he would be moved into a self-contained program[6]. The next day, predictably, he

---

[6] A self-contained program is one in which the student is isolated from the mainstream until they earn their way out of the self-contained program, through monitored and catalogued behavior modification.

did not show up for class so I put my students on "honor code" and went to the cafeteria to see if he was there. He was. He saw me coming and I could see his anger building as I approached him. There wasn't much else I could do at this point except to stand alongside him and very quietly ask if he would please come with me. There was no way that he was going to do that though. Instead he stood up and became very disrespectful.

At this point he was standing alongside me, so I moved to position myself facing sideways, but right in front of him, and asked him very simply: "Have I ever done or said anything to you that was ever disrespectful in any way?" He made eye contact with me and said "no". I repeated my request for him to come with me to talk a little bit about what was going on.

He reluctantly agreed and we walked to my classroom, but we did not go in the room as I knew it could be way too awkward for him to do so at that moment. Instead, I sat on the floor against the lockers outside my classroom and asked him to sit on the floor alongside me. It took some calm encouragement, but he reluctantly sat down. It was obvious he was still reeling about what was decided in the meeting the day before, so I addressed that issue right away.

I knew this student needed immediate validation, and I knew that whatever I said in that moment had to be as powerful as I could possibly make it. I told him that I knew how he was feeling about the decisions being made for him, how frustrating that meeting must have been, and that I would be pissed off too. I also told him that I understood why he didn't come to class and if it had been me, I probably wouldn't have come to school at all that day.

What he really needed to hear though, was that one of the reasons he was placed in my class was because there were people in the building who wanted us to meet. Then I told him there was a reason we should work together, saying: "when I was your age I was one pissed off kid at this high school too, so pissed off in fact, that I dropped out in my senior year".

Now I rarely drop that bombshell in my first encounter with a student, but I knew I had to make a meaningful connection with him right away. He looked at me and I said: "I dropped out because I was pissed off at everything and everyone including my alcohol abusing mother and abusive father, but there was nobody for me to turn to, and that is why some people wanted us to meet."

He never cut our Resource class again. At the end of the school year he said that our meeting in the hall was the "craziest meeting [he'd] ever had with a teacher." I was rewarded by his candor and his recognition of the impact our meeting had on him. The last time he came to see me he was starting his sophomore year at Northern Michigan University.

Ultimately, most students realize that a special services placement is a positive intervention and they will benefit from more structure and monitoring and classes designed to meet the needs of students who are experiencing learning, behavioral and/or emotional issues.

Many of these students are eventually grateful and relieved to know that there are people in their high school to support them through the educational process. The Resource Program has become instrumental in that process by providing a supportive environment where students can learn more about themselves, and where they can receive the support that will help to improve their academic achievement.

As I help my students through these transitions I also encourage them to put their perception of the placement and its accompanying label into perspective. I try to help them acknowledge that the direction they are moving in is positive; that they are finally going to get the support they deserve. Still, it is often a difficult transition. After all, who wants to be labeled?

I wish there were a better way but, institutionally, educationally and legally this is our system for placement. As educators and administrators we do our best to mitigate the negative impact a placement can have on a student in the short term, but it is still a difficult process.

Despite the challenges, a placement gives students an opportunity to receive multiple levels of support services throughout their educational experience, culminating in the completion of their graduation requirements and being awarded their high school diploma. So the difficult process has a pay-off, thankfully.

$\mathcal{A}$ $\mathcal{G}$ROWING $\mathcal{U}$RGENCY

$\mathcal{I}$ knew a man who was incredibly intelligent, who had built himself a small empire in the commercial real estate business. He was the sort of man known to proclaim his wealth aloud, bragging about his two hundred and fifty million dollar worth and professional superiority to those around him. But this man, so successful in his professional life, was also in and out of rehabilitation programs for decades throughout his adult life. This business tycoon, worth so many millions, ultimately lost his home, his wife, his business partner, and the respect of his children, due to his issues with substance abuse and his difficulties with successful rehabilitation.

Later in his life he hired a group of musicians and formed a small band in which he was the clarinet player. The band would travel to nursing homes, playing music for the elderly residents. After his shows, this man often returned to his hotel room, only to pour himself into a bottle.

This may seem like a strange story. Why did he neglect and finally walk away from his business and his family? How did this brilliant, talented and successful business-man become so lost in substance abuse and its subsequent consequences?

Why did this man end up playing music in homes for the elderly?

In my opinion he did so because he was searching for greater meaning, purpose and fulfillment in his life. I don't think he ever found it, largely because he never ad-dressed the core issues that were driving his self-defeating thoughts, emotions and behaviors. He never recognized the importance of emotional intelligence and was never able to successfully forgive himself of his failings.

I often cite his story in my classroom when I am talk-ing to my students about the differences between mate-rial success and emotional fulfillment. One can achieve financial or material success and still live a life filled with failures. Without building a strong sense of mean-ing and purpose in one's life, even the wealthiest of peo-ple can find it difficult to achieve feelings of personal satisfaction and emotional fulfillment.

When we lack a sense of meaning in our lives, life can become very difficult; especially if we don't take advan-tage of the opportunities to make necessary changes that will lead to a sense of positive self-worth and personal val-ue. These are the feelings of fulfillment that were missing in this businessman-turned-musician's life; but since he was never honest with himself about the issues he faced, he ended up denying himself that chance for fulfillment. Instead he became an alcohol abuser and passed away due to heart disease at a relatively young age.

Everyone wants to generate meaning and purpose in their lives. We all want to be satisfied with our achievements and fulfilled by our accomplishments. However, despite these common desires, sometimes we still find that our successes feel hollow or are lacking in purpose. It is at these times that life can become a little tricky if we are not honest with ourselves.

In these moments, if we ignore those feelings that something is lacking, if we dismiss what our hearts are telling us in an effort to avoid facing certain hard realities about ourselves, we can fall into patterns that become increasingly difficult to break. If we deceive ourselves into believing that all is well, when in reality all is not well because something important is missing, then we deny ourselves the opportunity to grow in purpose and fulfillment.

What is missing in these moments is what I consider "authentic living"—or living truthfully. But if we take the time and energy to work towards finding meaning and purpose in our lives, we will start to experience the benefits of authentic living.

In recent years, when I am in the classroom working with my students, I find myself noticing a greater sense of urgency than ever before. Many of my students already live in poverty or in homes where the income is nearing the poverty level—and this reality is much bigger than poverty as defined by mere economic terms.

While many of my students struggle with economic poverty, there is a certain poverty of the spirit that they are struggling with as well. They are dealing with complex and challenging social, educational and familial situations; and the experiences they have in these settings directly impact both their decisions about the way they live and their employability.

Collectively, we often perpetuate the notion that opportunities will become available to those who work hard enough—and I still believe that sentiment holds some element of truth—but for too many young people our society functions within a systemic set of beliefs and practices designed to disable them from accessing opportunities to create positive change in their lives. It is scary to think about the limitations that society will place on these young people if they don't find a way to change their thoughts and actions, and transcend their immediate situation.

Too many of the young people I teach, because of their struggles with social and emotional issues, have not always been available learners in the classroom, and consequently have not maximized their educational opportunities. These dynamics often lead to a gap between what they have learned and what society expects them to have learned.

The world in which my students are entering the workforce has become more competitive than ever, as economic systems have become more globalized and the academic and professional achievements required for successful, sustainable employment are becoming more and more demanding. Employers can afford to be more selective in the current economic structures, because middle class employment opportunities are increasingly scarce and the number of individuals competing for them is high.

I can list a few examples: as our manufacturing sector continues to adjust to a changing environment, prospective employers have become much more selective in their hiring practices, creating greater competition for the jobs that are available. This is partly due to the fact that increasing productivity through advanced technology has resulted in the need for fewer workers on a production floor: a significant cause for the slump in manufacturing job growth.

In another market for employment, the food service industry, there is an increase of competition between younger and older workers—specifically senior citizens who are seeking any employment available to them in a weak job market, due to a need to supplement their retirement incomes and secure basic employer-sponsored health insurance.

We'll have to wait and see how the Affordable Care Act addresses health care access and costs, but until we get to a single payer or a Medicare for All system, workers—and especially older workers—are going to continue to struggle to meet their health care needs if employer health plans are not available to them. As a result, recent graduates are going to have to struggle in a job market that is even more saturated with individuals competing for employment.

Many of my students are also facing a new paradigm regarding how unemployment rates are quantified in this country. Economists used to interpret and quantify full employment as a rate at which around only four or five percent of the population remained unemployed. I believe it is possible that with the structural changes we are experiencing today in our changing economic systems and patterns of economic growth, unemployment rates of closer to six percent will be accepted as full employment.

We also have to face the fact that unemployment rates are often misreported and misrepresented by mainstream print and broadcast media. For example, studies and reports issued by the Bureau of Labor Statistics present the statistical averages of unemployment rates, across all demographics. The national media almost always reports *only* these overall averages, which too often ignore the unemployment rates of minorities and teens. Unemployment rates are not static. They are, however, stubborn which often negatively affects younger and minority groups.

As of June, 2015, the Bureau of Labor Statistics reports the following unemployment rates:

Demographic	Unemployment Rate (%)
African American	9.5%
Caucasian	4.2%

Now, let's compare those rates with the rates of African American and Caucasian teens:

Demographic	Unemployment Rate (%)
African American <20	31.8%
Caucasian <20	15.7%

Not only do these unemployment rates differ greatly when age is included in the demographic profile, but on the whole the percentages of those unemployed are astounding; and they have been at these rates for way too long. Given current economic forces, familial dysfunction, and educational opportunities, there seems to be few viable solutions in sight.

Another negative impact on the employability of young people today is the growing use of personality tests in making hiring decisions. Companies ranging from those of the food service industry and big box retailers, to those jobs requiring prospective hires to have completed a college degree, have begun implementing personality tests as one facet of their hiring process. Many of these tests were first conducted in the early part of the twentieth century, but the personality tests being used today have been refined to reflect the "science" of what is now commonly referred to as human analytics that seek to define cognitive, behavioral, and cultural traits. The purported purpose of these rather sophisticated instruments is to identify factors that are supposed to predict a prospective employee's success. These tests have become a significant factor in determining the hiring decisions of many companies' human resource departments.

In "How High is Your XQ: Your Next Job Might Depend On It" (*TIME*, June 2015) staff writer Eliza Gray, reports that in fact, a $2 billion dollar industry has grown from the design and implementation of personality tests, which, on the whole, are supposed to serve to "fight employee turnover, increase productivity and improve customer satisfaction", without taking into consideration the needs of the employees themselves.

I have sat with some of my students as they have tried to complete online job applications, in which personality tests have been integral to the process, and it is daunting.

I have observed young people trying to complete applications of one or two hundred questions—which are used to predict the desirability of a candidate, and their likelihood of meeting the expectations of an employer—but the process is simply not designed in a way that encourages candidate success, and the experience can be quite unsettling for these young people.

For example, some of my students have applied to a regional fast food chain, and others to a regional retail store, and submitting a personality profile has been a requirement of the application process. My teenage students who are trying to secure a part time job are asked "true or false" questions like, as Eliza Gray reports: "I never get angry," "my parents praised me for my achievements," "when I was young, there were times when I felt like leaving home," "I dislike the high taxes we have to pay in this country," or "sometimes I'm not sure what I really believe." Not only are such questions not necessarily applicable to the manner in which a young person would behave in the work place, they are confusing for the student as well. My students look to me, wondering what these questions have to do with busing tables or stocking inventory. I do my best to calm them down as they struggle to get through the process.

These are just some of the factors that challenge or contribute to delays in a young person's entry into the work force; an issue which only further challenges their employability because of the chronological gap it creates. An eighteen or nineteen year old who has not yet established a work record will likely have a harder time getting a job than his or her peers who entered the workforce in an entry-level or part-time position at fifteen or sixteen.

Prospective employers are much more likely to hire an applicant who *has* established a work history than one who hasn't worked before.

We need to realize that poverty really does concern much more than basic income and overall economic conditions. We have to take into consideration all the issues that lead to poverty—negative dynamics in a student's personal, educational and professional life, cultural, social and generational economic conditions, compounded by the expectations society has imposed upon them—before we might truly understand how to help people escape the systemic, institutionalized discrimination that can lead to living as part of the permanent underclass—beneath or near the U.S. poverty line—and how to prevent our young people from entering it.

But please know this too, it is not just those who have struggled economically who are at risk of living as part of the permanent underclass.

As I observe the changing economic dynamics of the United States, I am often reminded of the fact that dysfunction knows no economic barrier. I witness the manifestation of this fact in the students I teach every day, and I know this from my own life, as my family was not necessarily economically disadvantaged, though our familial dysfunction was profound.

I have worked with some of the most emotionally disturbed adolescents, so many of whom, despite significant economic wealth (driving to school in dad's $80,000 luxury car, for example) were terribly disturbed. In my classroom, students who are a part of the state-assisted lunch program are sitting next to classmates who come from families of significant, upper-class economic wealth.

It is amazing to witness how often the emotional disturbances shared amongst these adolescents find them on common ground when it comes to emotional management and better decision making—even though economically, they live worlds apart. It often gives some of my wealthier students a moment for pause, if I mention my hope that their nicest car will not be the last one their parents purchase for them. The reality is that when the economic apron strings are cut, these young people are going to face many similar challenges to those of their less economically-advantaged peers—regarding furthering their educational opportunities, their employability, and their emotional management skills going forward. They too are going to have to sit down and take a personality test.

Again, dysfunction knows no economic barrier. The students whose stories I have shared in this book do not necessarily come from economically disadvantaged families—some of them have come from extremely affluent families, and attend school in what is reputed to be a largely affluent community. These students are members of what has become known as the "1%" of the United States—and while their economic affluence can certainly be a huge advantage when it comes to furthering their education, or becoming gainfully employed—it is not necessarily a huge advantage when developing healthy emotional management skills. I also work with plenty of students who find themselves somewhere in the middle of these two economic extremes—students whose families live comfortably within their middle class means, but who also struggle with their own lack of emotional intelligences, and making consistent, self-enhancing decisions that will lead to living productive, meaningful lives.

The reality of wealth, or general economic comfort, is that it guarantees nothing—even though many think that it does. I have often witnessed parents struggling with the belief that: "I have given my child everything; how could this have happened?" Sometimes, we forget that economic affluence is only one type of wealth—there are a myriad of ways to be wealthy, and all offer some benefit, some even more than that of material wealth.

Mother Theresa, for example, who lived most of her life in the Calcutta region of India as religious sister and missionary, often talked about the different poverties she witnessed. She was often quoted as speaking about material poverty, versus spiritual poverty—and not necessarily spiritual poverty as it relates to religion, but simply an overall personal sense of emotional well-being. Once, when talking about the differences between the United States, a country of obvious material wealth, and her home of Calcutta, often cited as the poorest city on the planet, she said: "The spiritual poverty of the Western World is much greater than the physical poverty of our people. You, in the West, have millions of people who suffer such terrible loneliness and emptiness. They feel unloved and unwanted. These people are not hungry in the physical sense, but they are in another way. They know they need something more than money, yet they don't know what it is." A harsh, but accurate assessment of the world we live in, no?

As frustrating as it is to witness the dysfunctional decision making and poor emotional management skills of my students, what becomes even more difficult to navigate is the belief that one's economic affluence, or lack thereof, somehow prevents dysfunction. Coming from, as I mentioned, what is reputed to be a school of extremely affluent students—and often this is the case—I have heard time and time again the disbelief that: "you have kids like *that* at your high school?" Kids like "*that*", meaning, the at-risk students.

As my sense of urgency, regarding the future well-being of my students, has intensified, I have become far less tolerant towards the kind of ignorance and insincerity that leads someone to believe that a wealthy student will be immune from the dysfunction, disappointments, and emotional pitfalls of life. This is why I offer the perspective that no one individual, nor any one family, regardless of economic advantages or disadvantages, is free from the challenges of raising an at-risk youth. Instead it is important to realize that all children share certain vulnerabilities: they are fallible human beings who can fall victim to dysfunctional beliefs and behaviors just like any other child or adolescent, regardless of which "side of the tracks" they come from. We all put our pants on one leg at a time.

In other words, this is not just about money. It concerns a mindset informed by one's beliefs about themselves and the world around them. Systemic poverty is a cultural and an educational concern as well as an economic one. Culture and education are powerful forces and society can be very unforgiving when it comes to making value judgments of a person and his or her potential. Coming from the "wrong side of the tracks", so to speak, can still be very problematic for a lot of young people.

How then, do I approach the daunting task of trying to both heal and prepare my students for the future challenges that each one of them is going to face? I focus my work on thought-based beliefs. This is critical in nurturing their ability to live up to their potential. This speaks to the fundamental question: *what kind of a life do you want for yourself?*

Again: it is our self-talk that determines our emotional reactions and behavioral responses to life's events. Self-talk is our processing tool—informing how we interact with ourselves, others and the world around us. It guides us through our daily experiences, and tells us how to behave.

Remember the diagram of this cognitive process?

THOUGHTS
create
EMOTIONS
that result in
BEHAVIORS

This idea of the cognitive behavioral model didn't just begin with Dr. Ellis and his model of Rational Emotive Behavior Therapy and Education either. History is filled with leaders and thinkers who were interested in the link between cognitive processes. Here are just a few examples:

- Epictetus: "Men are not disturbed by things but by their view of them."
- Marcus Aurelius: "The happiness of your life depends on the quality of your thoughts."
- The Buddha: "We are what we think. With our thoughts we make the world."
- Shakespeare: There is nothing either good or bad but thinking makes it so."
- The Bible: "As a man thinketh in his heart, so is he."

In my own classroom, personal empowerment is one of my main focuses when trying to help students realize that they can transcend environmental circumstances by re-conditioning themselves to engage in more self-enhancing and productive ways of thinking and behaving. Understanding this process is everyone's best chance at changing ineffective and self-defeating patterns of thinking and behaving.

$\mathcal{C}$ONNECTING
$\mathcal{T}$EACHING &
$\mathcal{P}$ARENTING

$\mathcal{O}$ ne of the most moving and memorable teaching experiences I have had happened on the last day of a Health class I taught. I was having a conversation with two of my most at-risk students about what they valued most about my class and one of them said "I was touched when you talked about fatherhood." It may not sound like much, but this was a powerful moment, hearing those words coming from this particular young man.

He was one of the most disenfranchised young people I have ever taught, and he was telling me that he had been "touched" by something I had taught him. That word blew me away. *Touched*? This kind of expression just isn't often spoken aloud by a student like him; given his racial, social and economic background. It was not part of the lexicon one would expect from this student, and yet here he was expressing it.

I knew my Health class was enjoying our discussions, in part, because it was one class that most of them never ditched. Most students who enroll in one of the content courses I teach end up attending that class noticeably more than their other classes. This is largely due to my personal philosophy, my teaching methodology and the expectations I establish each time I interact with a student.

But it is more than that. My effectiveness is grounded in my passion for what I do; for the awesome responsibility with which I have been entrusted. My goal is to engage and guide my students toward becoming more active learners and toward healthier living.

As a teacher, when moments of personal realization occur they can be profoundly moving experiences, in part because they have been brought on by a teenager I've worked with. So for parents, when you're honest with yourselves, able to relax your constraints and set aside the ego-driven issues reflected in your own expectations, you'll better notice those moments when your teenager has had a positive, encouraging impact on you.

When you look at your child in a new light, because you realize they are coming into their own, it is a powerful experience. The challenge is being able to accept their individual growth in those moments when you may personally disagree with them. When you are able to admit that you are proud, even if you don't necessarily agree, is a bonding experience for both of you because you are able to validate their growth and they are able to validate your parenting.

The result is encouragement in the direction of independence, verses turning your child into who you believe they must become. Loosening the parental reins can be very difficult for some parents, but if you have instilled the moral compass you hoped to instill in your child by the time they have entered high school, then you can begin to pull back. This is not to say you don't parent your teenager. To the contrary, you are better able to parent without as many power struggles.

The relationship model for effective teaching is just as effective for parenting. But it's not building a friendship that I'm talking about. I am still the teacher and you are still the parent. The model is based on a healthy relationship built on a foundation of respect. When a teenager realizes the relationship with their teacher or parent is based on respect for who they are as an individual, they are better able to strengthen their sense of respect for themselves.

We all know that self-respect is one cornerstone of effective decision making and productive living. When a teenager experiences such a realization it is very empowering. It is also a very rewarding growth for both parent and teacher.

Parenting and teaching both offer similar rewards and growth experiences. In many ways educators take on a parenting role in our classrooms. These growth experiences occur frequently, if you are truly listening and watching. One must be patient and careful not to take student input for granted, or to be dismissive because their input doesn't fit in with what you were trying to accomplish.

Body language is critical at these times too. We must be attentive to any subtleties in our students' behaviors, and present for what these subtleties may indicate about how a student is thinking or feeling. We can't be looking at the clock, or down at our desk, or shuffling papers. Growth as a parent and growth as a teacher comes in daily doses through patience, presence, humility, the relaxation of our constraints and by being as non-judgmental as possible.

The formal learning process should never be taken for granted either, nor should we ever think that we have learned all that we need to learn. There is always room for growth, and in the field of education this is well recognized. Growth through continuing education is invaluable: parenting classes, self-help books, counseling, continuing education classes, degree programs and the like are just a few examples.

For teachers there are many educational requirements and opportunities for continued professional growth. It is a commitment that continues throughout one's career, which can span decades. A teacher's education does not end with receiving a teaching certificate. District administrators, school boards and many state boards of education require continuing education of their teaching staff.

In addition to my formal education, many of my most important professional growth experiences have occurred in the classroom. No amount of training and education can prepare you for some of the more moving experiences that occur there. So the young man in my health class was "touched" and so was I.

LESSON 8: WHERE DO I GO FROM HERE?

I have described some of the more basic principles of Dr. Ellis's therapeutic model of Rational Emotive Behavior Therapy (REBT) and later Rational Emotive Behavior Education (REBE) that stemmed from his frustrating years of practicing traditional psychotherapy, which he concluded was not effectively addressing the cognitive and emotional disturbances he was witnessing in his patients.

In response he set out to develop a brand of cognitive behavioral therapy and education that would attack the irrational and distorted thought processes of his patients through the use of Socratic questioning as well as the more direct approach of didactic strategies, replacing irrational beliefs with more rational and effective ways of thinking.

His efforts were both rewarded and thwarted. They were rewarded through a movement that understood the essence of effective therapy, and they were thwarted by the established leaders and thinkers in psychology who saw his methodology as too simplistic. But the establishment also recognized REBT as a threat to the traditional psychotherapeutic practices already in place. Ellis's efforts were also diminished by those who took exception to the revolutionary nature of his REBT model, as well as his forceful delivery and blunt approach (he cursed a lot). Despite the critics, Ellis's model of Rational Emotive Behavior Therapy survived and today the Ellis Institute continues his work from their headquarter offices in New York City and satellite operations in Chicago.

⌒

*M*y hope for this book is that it offers readers a glimpse of what can be achieved when we view our cognitive and emotional disturbances as an internal issue, by understanding that we each have a choice between living our lives through the lens of an external locus of control or an internal locus of control.

The former leads us to view ourselves as victim to the events that occur in our lives, while the latter affords us greater control over how we react to those events, thereby giving us more individual control over our thoughts, emotions and behaviors. As you practice some of these cognitive strategies and integrate the philosophies, principles and practices of REBT/E into your life, the quality of your life will improve.

I have shared some of my own life experiences for context, in hopes of offering a deeper meaning to what I have written in this book. It is up to each of us to decide if we want to take charge of our lives by being in charge of our reactions, or whether we want to be controlled by external events. The choice is ours to make. The decisions over how we choose to live our lives are truly up to us.

My students realize the lifelong benefit of what I teach. They see it as something they have never been exposed to before: the idea that they could learn skills and strategies that would give them greater control over their thoughts, emotions and behaviors and thereby greater control of their lives. If we were to dedicate more effort in the area of emotional intelligence it would have a profound impact on our abilities to gain greater control and accept greater accountability over the decisions we make in our lives.

We cannot ignore the advantages of living authentically. But recognizing the importance of doing so doesn't just magically happen, especially to young people. Living authentically is essential to achieving what most of us strive for: self-fulfillment and the sense of contentment that comes with it.

I hope this book will help inspire you to change your thinking in order to limit negative decision-making and self-defeating emotions and behavior. I hope you will make a commitment to continue your education in the area of REBT/E so that you can strengthen the skills which will lead you closer to living an authentic life. Remember that your quest to live authentically ultimately comes from you and it begins with the way you choose to think, emote and behave.

But know this too: while this reading may be your first entrée into the kind of self-exploration that is necessary to begin anew, it won't end here. It is going to require a redundancy of practice and your own persistence to get better at thinking about your thinking. I hope that in some way I have contributed to improving the lives of young people by advancing the principles of REBT/E as a classroom teacher and author.

All it takes is an intentional examination of your core philosophy and your beliefs about yourself, others and the world around you. Begin the process of adopting healthier ways of thinking, emoting and behaving. Let me leave you with a self-talk rallying cry:

"I will not be beaten.
I will not be defeated.
I will not be conquered; not even by myself."

CONCLUSION

*I*t has been extraordinarily rewarding to realize that my hypothesis, the driving force from the beginning of my journey to become a teacher, was accurate. Essentially what I believed was that my students could find meaning in learning from a teacher who survived the challenges of being raised in a violently dysfunctional family; a teacher who had dropped out of high school and who had learned how to overcome the fear and failure that that kind of adversity foments.

I was convinced that my life experiences could set me apart from any teacher they had ever known. I believed that because of my own struggles I could make an essential connection with these students that would help them gain greater insight and find deeper meaning in their lives, and that they could recognize the inner strength that comes from their own struggles.

I believed I could guide them toward greater self-awareness and self-confidence—to help students understand that they too can survive and grow up to live fulfilling lives. I believed students could gain a greater sense of themselves and develop the resources needed to access their inner strength by seeing and hearing for themselves that I survived. I also believed my experiences would give them encouragement and a fresh perspective.

My goal was, and remains, to guide young people to a greater understanding of themselves and the world around them—to help them recognize that their adversity must become a source of strength. If they don't recognize the tremendous potential that surviving adversity offers, the opposite will be the case: their adversity will become a source of weakness which will only perpetuate a potentially endless cycle of self-defeating beliefs and behaviors.

Dysfunction really thrives by feeding on itself. Dysfunctional behavior is not something that we're born with; it is learned behavior through the adoption of certain beliefs and values stemming from family dynamics, social and economic class, cultural orientation, ethnicity, race and education.

The key to my success with at-risk students is the unique level of authenticity that I bring to the classroom and the purpose and meaning this authenticity creates within the classroom experience. The meaning that students assign to hearing about how my struggles can relate to their own lives is powerful, but even more empowering is seeing the meaning I ascribe to those struggles as I look back on them now.

It gives students both comfort and confidence to know that they too can survive and grow up to live a fulfilling life. Most gain some measure of strength by seeing and hearing for themselves that I not only survived but that I also achieved my goals. Our discussions also offer them the idea that they too can find their inner-self and inner-strength, and the hope for the future that belief in oneself accords.

Daily life for many of these students is fundamentally dominated by the stress of maintaining both defensive and offensive survival strategies. Unfortunately, they are not well equipped to meet the challenges of poverty, broken family structures and drug and alcohol abuse that many of them and their friends and families face.

For many of my students the result of being in a long term and/or constant state of fear and uncertainty often results in being diagnosed with post-traumatic stress disorder, depression, obsessive compulsive disorder, conduct disorders, behavioral/emotional disorders, generalized anxiety, thought disorders and personality disorders.

Compounding their challenges is the fact that most of these teenagers are enmeshed in issues of generational poverty and the broken family structures that such poverty often causes. The result is that they don't receive the kind of nurturance, guidance and structure that would give them a fighting chance at breaking the cycle.

Sometimes though, their inner spirit or innate abilities defy the influences of their experiences with dysfunctional families, negative and self-defeating social relationships and chronic underachievement. The human spirit is amazing in its resiliency, and this is apparent in my students' reaction to honest, authentic exchanges of ideas and experiences. It is a gripping experience when at-risk students step away from the pathologies that have grown from their environments, to share an honest and functional thought or feeling.

In creating an effective learning environment I can facilitate the learning opportunities that lead to positive outcomes in students' lives. Over time my classroom has reflected an ongoing, multi-faceted dynamic; the basis of which is the connection between the reality of my student's experiences and the impact I have on challenging their tendency to fall victim to that reality. It was that realization that also resulted in my commitment to writing this book.

As I look back on my life before teaching, it amazes me that it took as much soul searching as it did, and over so many years, to accept the fact that for me to be true to myself, and to realize my potential (beyond making money), I had to make a career change. I had to teach, but, as you know, I had to teach students who were a lot like me when I was their age.

I wanted to try and reduce the incidence of people becoming part of the permanent underclass that is growing in our country because so many young people don't have the cognitive strategies and emotional skills to avoid being sucked into the morass of irrational beliefs about themselves and their world conditions.

When sharing my own life experiences of growing up in a large family that struggled with depression, alcohol abuse and brutal domestic violence, I came to realize that this sharing was key to giving greater import to the idea of those experiences being tapped as sources of inner strength.

It might seem surprising that a child who came from a troubled home, who wasn't a good student and who dropped out of high school decided to become a teacher, right? But there was something that transcended those issues and challenges, and that was the extraordinary impact a handful of teachers had on me over those early years of my schooling.

I was lucky enough to have teachers filled with compassion; teachers who were wholly dedicated to their profession and to their students—not just as students, but as individuals with varying academic, social, and emotional skills.

Life changing teachers are not taught; they're born. This speaks to instincts as well as inherent ability. This speaks to knowing the incredible value of the empathetic, relational aspects of teaching that I believe are inherent in effective teachers. Teachers cut from this cloth are the ones who exemplify the essence of the master teacher. These are the people whose impact is far reaching and everlasting.

$\mathcal{A}$CKNOWLEDGEMENTS

$\mathcal{I}$n a sense the origin of this book is in the people whose lives intertwined with mine. Their influence, both positive and negative, contributed to all that I have accomplished. I have concluded that my life experiences, through the challenges that were mine to overcome, were not just random events or coincidences but meaningful occurrences that I had to engage, interpret, and define in order to give meaning to how I would live my life.

It was ultimately the decisions I had to make from my field of choices, which were going to offer me some reasonable level of meaning and purpose. So I must acknowledge each of the people discussed in this book as those who inspired, guided, and supported me.

To my wife Jeanne, I am forever grateful. Without your love and devotion I may not have survived long enough to become a teacher and author. It is because of your unwavering support of my quest to change careers, undaunted by the risks, which led to my becoming a teacher. Without your determination, guidance, and continuous support this book would not have been completed. It was a difficult challenge to revisit my childhood experiences, but your wisdom, insights, and strength of purpose led to this book's completion. You are the love of my life and I thank you from the bottom of my heart.

To my third grade teacher Sister Mary, and my sophomore speech teacher Molly, I give thanks for the lasting impact their humanity and skill have had on me as a teacher.

There is also a long list of friends from Paul and David, my early childhood friends, to John, Ken, Darlene, Terry, Deb and Dean whose commitment to our friendship has and continues to strengthen me. I thank you too for tolerating my indulgences.

To Jack and Ellen, my business partners, I am truly amazed by your faith in my skills and inherent talents that brought us together to advance our collective achievements. I thank you for your support and patience, as I know it wasn't always easy.

There are times that present opportunities when we only have a moment to act. On the last day of school in 1999 I had one such moment. I was saying goodbye to a student who I had helped shepherd through high school. I offered my farewell, but as she walked away from our classroom I decided to stop her to tell her how special she was and that I hoped she would stay in touch. She did, and our friendship continues to this day. Thank you, Elizabeth, for your commitment to our friendship. It is, just like you, very special and I am most grateful to have you in my life.

Last but not least, I must thank Jeff, my mentor and friend without whom I would not be the teacher I am today. I reflect often on the wisdom that grew from your thirty-nine years of teaching and I am eternally grateful for your willingness to accept and mentor me for all the years we worked side-by-side. Together we helped guide some of the most disillusioned, disenfranchised, down-trodden and alienated young people within our school setting toward healthier and more meaningful and productive living.

$\mathcal{A}$BOUT THE $\mathcal{A}$UTHOR

William J. Palmer is a special education teacher at Barrington High School in suburban Chicago, the same school from which he dropped out before earning a diploma. He would go on to earn a GED, and multiple academic degrees including a master of arts in special education from Northeastern Illinois University.

Before returning to teach at Barrington, Palmer had a successful career in commercial real estate. He recognized his true calling, however, as one who could both empathize with and inspire at-risk youth. Palmer specializes in teaching young people with behavior and emotional difficulties as he emphasizes the connections between negative personal experiences and the potential for academic failure. He seeks to help young people overcome the challenges of growing-up in fractured family structures sometimes compromised further by economic difficulties, alcohol abuse, or domestic violence, and help other educators inspire positivity in their classrooms.

Made in the USA
Lexington, KY
29 May 2016